BIG WHEELS RANCH

BIG WHEELS RANCH

Catherine Camp

River Sanctuary
PUBLISHING

Cover and interior photos provided by Catherine Camp
Pen-and-ink illustrations by Sally NeSmith

ISBN 978-1-935914-88-4

Available from:
RiverSanctuaryPublishing.com
Amazon.com

Printed in the United States of America

RIVER SANCTUARY PUBLISHING
P.O Box 1561
Felton, CA 95018
www.riversanctuarypublishing.com
Dedicated to the awakening of the New Earth

Contents

INTRODUCTION

Writing about your own life is complicated and a little presumptuous. Writing about people you love and a place you love, people you are living with, people who may be the ones to help when you get even older and weirder, is also an intimidating undertaking. I am writing here about living through interesting and, sometimes, tumultuous times. It is also about a place I love, Big Wheels Ranch, and my own long connection with it. It is a story about family, a specific 40 acres, the times we have lived, about sharing a grand adventure.

This work is also about growing up, or growing old, and growing together. In the times I write most about, we were young and the storms of love and bad decisions and disappointing politics were new and upsetting. Passions often raged, in love and in anger. The ranch and the larger community reflected all the drama. Aging has let me see all that I owe friends and co-conspirators, bringing me to recognize that everyone needs understanding and, sometimes, forgiveness. Our lives individually are not so stormy today, although we are not immune to illness, disability, heartbreak, death. At this distance, it is easier to recognize our interdependence, our mutual indebtedness, and the joy of a long journey taken together.

The stories that follow are not an autobiography, exactly. They are not even a history of tumultuous times, although the political and cultural storms of the last nearly fifty years are characters that we will see in some of the stories. Most of all, the optimism and commitment of our time have something to offer toward meeting today's challenges, I hope. The stories are also not intended to be a history of Big Wheels Ranch, or a how-to book for communards. Taken together, the stories are closer to a memoir of my connection to this place, those times, and these people.

1

The first chapter, Growing Up, provides a history of my own relationship with Big Wheels Ranch. I also explore the political tumults of the late twentieth century as I experienced them. Finally, I talk about how those tumults affected my courtship and marriage. The second chapter, Growing Family, tells the story of forming the ranch, learning to live together, and confronting challenges. The Women's Movement, Gay Pride, and Aging all played, and continue to play, a major role in our time together. Chapter 3, Growing Land, is an effort to talk about the larger neighborhood in all its glories and challenges. At a time when rural parts of this country are changing rapidly, the history and reality of this very specific place have something to tell.

The times have changed, and perhaps we have all made less difference than we thought we might. Indeed, in these newly changing and terrifying times, we are all assessing the state of community. But here in this place and in this time we find ourselves with a beautiful home place, healthy children, strong relationships with each other, and some stories to tell.

Chapter 1
Growing Up

Persons attempting to find a motive in this narrative will be prosecuted; persons attempting to find a moral in it will be banished; persons attempting to find a plot in it will be shot.

By Order of the Author

Mark Twain, *Adventures of Huckleberry Finn*

At no point can the world stop spinning on its axis long enough for us to say with certainty, 'This is the way it is.' The only constancy is change. Within the present chapter of history there is still movement. Our new community in this particular 'somewhere' has already experienced several births, a few deaths, and many changes in mating partners. Each year we notice that the stream beds have altered their courses and the ocean has taken sand from the beaches or caused new slides along the bluffs. Numerous buildings and roads and gardens exist today that didn't exist a few years ago, and several abandoned cars and campsites give witness to our fluidity.

Ray Raphael, *An Everyday History of Somewhere*

BEGINNINGS

On Christmas Eve in the early 1970s, I packed hostess gifts of wine and a beautiful wooden salad bowl, along with my three-year-old, Ben, into my battered yellow Mustang. Although I am not a sporty car girl, the used Mustang had been a present from my recently-ex-husband. The gift was one of several futile efforts by both of us to hold the marriage together. The weather looked threatening, but I donned a floor-length patchwork dress-up skirt, dangly peace earrings, and knee-high boots. As Ben and I drove up into the mountains, the rain became heavier, turning to snow about ten miles from my destination. The smart thing to do would have been to turn around. I had been raised in Southern California; I had no experience driving in snow, no chains, and only a hazy notion of how dangerous this all was. But if I turned around, where would I go? Back to my dark, empty apartment? On Christmas Eve?

I could see the end of my twenties, and not in the distance, either. I had moved into a low-rent apartment with Ben, leaving the relative affluence and stable situation of marriage to a rising young professional. Somehow, the anger and pain of the marriage break-up sustained me through finding the apartment, finding a job, finding the lawyer to file the divorce, moving the furniture, settling in.

Once we were settled into our new abode, the full impact of my new life became clear. I had never lived alone. I'd gone directly from home to college dorm to married life. While living with a three-year-old was certainly not quiet, and not boring, it felt alone in all adult respects. Who would see to it that the oil was changed on the car? Who would share in, and celebrate, the making of a real dinner? Who would decide if the babysitter was up to the job of tending that precious boy? Each new challenge was a hill to climb, requiring strength and determination, often tears, and the presence of friends to encourage and provide suggestions. Was this struggle what being a grown-up was always going to be like?

A challenge that loomed bigger than most was what to do about holidays: especially, Christmas. Going home to Mom was always an option, but it would be hard to arrange shared Christmas time for Ben with my ex-husband if I went to the other end of the state. Mom didn't really approve of this divorce anyway. It just seemed to emphasize defeat, somehow, to go home. Joining any of my local friends with a standard two-parents-with-a-child family was possible, but felt like it would underscore how fragile and 'other' my life was now. So what about going up to Big Wheels Ranch?

I had just left the life of a stay-at-home mother, consisting of arranging the little dinner parties that signaled middle class success in the 1960's, and donating a few hours a week to teaching reading. I had a brand new job now – a loose assignment in administration of the local poverty program. For the first couple of months, my only contribution was to cry often and to show up every day. I suspected the agency paid me partly out of pity, partly in the hope those dinner party guests of yore would support local anti-poverty efforts on my behalf. Gradually, I was beginning to see a space for myself as I undertook the role of translating the efforts to implement the new Great Society programs into language the larger community could understand and accept. Some of my colleagues at the poverty program had just arranged to buy 40 acres of foothill land an hour east of town.

Big Wheels Ranch was named by its new owners for the 7-foot diameter wheels from a 1930s logging cart that graced a quarter-mile long dirt driveway. I had visited there a couple of times in the fall. The land was a lovely old homestead, with a log house built 50 years earlier, a year-round creek, a pasture with a barn, a sizeable apple orchard, and wooded areas covered with second-growth trees.

In this first year, the ranch was an intriguing and welcoming place. None of the participants had real experience with rural living.

But the California foothills are generally forgiving and the group was not, after all, expecting to live off the land. They were expecting to share resources, to reduce their consumption of consumer goods, and to provide a haven for folks who returned each day from work dealing with poverty and its attendant legal and social challenges. What better place on Christmas Eve for a fragile, but determined, single mother with her young child?

At the driveway to the ranch, my little car basically slid into a snow bank. It was dark; I had no flashlight; I had a whimpering three-year old who by now had figured out that Mom was scared; I had a bag full of presents; I was wearing a skirt. Crying myself by now, carrying Ben, I began to flounder through the snow toward the house, uncertain of anything except that I should not walk into any trees and fairly convinced that I could suffer great harm in this wilderness. A loud "Hello," just behind a flashlight, appeared in this dismal scene. It was Chris, the teenage son of my work supervisor Chuck, big and dressed in an even bigger wool coat. He had seen the headlights of my car. He dragged a sled behind him. "Here," he said, "put those presents on the sled, give me Ben for my shoulders, take my arm, and let's go see if the savages have left us any eggnog."

Housing at the ranch consisted of the 50-year-old main house, with its small and dark kitchen and single bath. The garage/tool shed had been remade into a very small house, and an even smaller structure called the chicken house could serve as a bedroom. From my current vantage point, it seems remarkable that 8 people lived in such a small indoor arrangement, especially sharing the kitchen and bath. On this holiday night, however, it was the warmest and most welcoming sight I could imagine. Log walls stained dusty red reflected the flames of a wood stove and the soft light of kerosene lamps (a holiday treat, as the ranch had electricity). A long wooden table, handmade by Chuck, was covered with mismatched thrift store dishes and greenery from the forest. A mouth-watering feast of turkey, salads, vegetables, and pie awaited. A lighted Christmas tree contained underneath a large and rustic wooden boat that Chris had made for Ben. It looked and felt like family to me.

I still had challenges to face as a single parent. The work I had chosen called on every bit of creativity and flexibility that I could muster. I probably needed a car that coped with the countryside better. But Ben and I found a fellowship that first Christmas, a warmth and comfort that became the hallmark of my future sojourns at the ranch.

WHERE ARE WE?

Big Wheels Ranch lies on the west side of the ridge of the Cascade mountain range in Northern California, roughly midway between the Shasta and Lassen peaks. The land around us is littered with signs of a long history of volcanic activity in the neighborhood. Underneath the sharp-edged volcanic evidence are layers of geology, millions of years of mountain-building, valley creating activities, each leaving evidence of change.

Driving to the ranch from Redding, one passes through a jumble of geologic stories in the rock. As the highway climbs east out of the Sacramento valley, road-cuts on the north side of the highway show dark slate and occasional outcrops of white limestone. Indeed, about halfway to the ranch turn-off there is a limestone quarry. Where did that limestone come from? It is made from the scrapings from the bottom of an ocean, compressed over a long period of time and scooped up by the movement of tectonic plates at the margin of North America into a continental mountain range. For the central part of the canyon that the highway passes through, the north-side rocks loom in an uneven wall, black and gray and white. These rocks are a jumbled mess of ocean sediments crushed as the continent moved west over the oceanic plate, roughly 200 million years ago.

The sediments were heated into metamorphic shapes and pushed back up as the Sierra Nevada range. The movement of the continent at this time happened because a ridge opened down the middle of the Atlantic Ocean, spreading apart and pushing the continental plate relentlessly west. The looming rocks should feel threatening; instead they just seem old. On the south side of the highway, the land is wild, but rocky and uneven, without the wall-like shape of the north side of the canyon. The road follows the course of a stream, Cow Creek, whose course has clearly been determined by the northern mountain block.

About 130 million years ago, the northern-most section of the Sierra Nevada mountains broke away from the rest of the range and moved west about 60 miles, to become known as the Klamath Mountains. The north side of the highway to the ranch is the southeastern edge of this Klamath block. The geology books I have read do not know why this jump happened. However, it opened a mostly landlocked seaway between the Klamath block and the Sierra range, the Modoc Seaway, that covered the land we now call our ranch. It was shallow and surrounded by mountains, so sediment began to fill it at a great rate.

The result of this very old break in the mountains is a sort of dividing line that the highway follows from Redding to Montgomery Creek, with the very old metamorphic rock on the north side, and a gentler series of hills and canyons on the south. The path of the highway is not precise, of course, but the feel of the land on each side of the highway is very different. The seaway to the south of the Klamath block has now been overlaid by much younger volcanic rocks. These are brownish and were spewed out over the last few million years as the Cascade mountains began to erupt. There are frequently erratic boulders that seem to have been blown over the landscape. Is it possible that the creek the highway follows is in fact the remnant of the seaway?

The most extravagant vision of the volcanic period is, of course, Mount Shasta to the north and Mount Lassen to the south. Both are visible as the highway leaves Redding, and they can be seen peeping over the hills occasionally, all the way to the summit of the Cascades in between them, Hatchet Mountain. Both peaks have erupted in the historic period, Mt. Shasta in 1786 and Mt. Lassen in 1914-1915. Both are likely to erupt again.

The land changes as the road emerges from the canyon about 20 miles east of Redding. About 30 million years ago, mountains that existed to the east and earlier than the Cascade range eroded due to rivers coursing off their slopes. Sometimes the rivers were rapid and tumbling, so that the rocks deposited in their curves were large. Sometimes the rivers were slower, the climate drier, and the rocks deposited when the land flattened out were small. The result is a sandstone layer underneath the volcanics of the Cascades, including on our land. The sandstone is impervious to water, and is called the Montgomery Creek formation.

As you near the ranch just east of the town of Montgomery Creek, there are outcrops of darker, blackish basalt, part of a volcanic event earlier than the rising of the current version of the Cascade mountains. About 17 million years ago, a very large center of volcanic activity opened in southeastern Oregon. Incredible lava flows poured southwest, covering the sediments from the Modoc Seaway and the Montgomery Creek formation with thick lava flows. When the volcanic basalt is visible, it is often dramatically layered and thick. The volcanic activity ended after 1.5 million years; the basalt flows are unlike anything else in the landscape. In most areas near the ranch, that basalt is covered with the more recent basalt, rhyolite and andesite of the Cascade volcanoes. When these more recent volcanic rocks are visible in road cuts or stream canyon walls, they are often layered, with blocky or rounded stones in between layers of smooth, light-colored ash. Layers are black or brown or pale.

In most places, of course, there is soil on top of this rocky story. The soil supports a pine and fir forest and our modest gardens, pasture, orchard, and house sites. The soil is the result of the inexorable erosion of the latest mountains, the Cascades. Creeks and rivers, rapid and slow, break down that basalt, rhyolite and andesite, helped along by freezing and warming, and the roots of trees and bushes and smaller plants.

So there you have it. Big Wheels ranch sits in the volcanic province of the Cascade mountain range. The layers of rock under our land and along our creeks include a ten mile thick column of rubble from a much earlier continental edge, 200 million years ago, the edge of the Klamath block Next comes a layer of sediment, the remnant of the Modoc Seaway dating to 130 million years ago. On top of that is a second layer of sedimentary sandstone, some with large cobbles and some with small, all of it impervious to water, the Montgomery Creek formation. In some parts of the area there are dark basalts, dating to the Oregon volcanic eruption of 17 million years ago. On top of it all is volcanic debris or basalt from two episodes of Cascade Range volcanic mountain building, one 10 million years ago with smooth flows, and one two million years ago with more explosive eruptions that produced Shasta and Lassen and their fellow Cascade peaks.

It all seems like myth-making, albeit entertaining myths. Continental tectonic plates shoulder aside or roll right over oceanic plates. A bulldozer as big as northern California scrapes up rubble from the seabed into mountain-range-sized piles along a moving coastline. Volatile mountains periodically erupt, leaving ash or liquid rock in pathways or flinging rocks about like children's blocks. Sometimes the results of the collisions, uprisings, and volcanic explosions fold over each other, so that the oldest rock might be on top of the younger in some places.

One result of this history is that water behaves in unpredictable ways at the ranch. Water flows through the rocky layers, whether that water is from springs or from septic systems. The water sinks only as deep as the Montgomery Creek formation of sandstone, where it seeks another outlet, up or down. As a result we find springs, which at our ranch provide our drinking water. Hot springs along the Pit River nearby are more evidence of the layered rock underneath this land. It is likely that water there seeps through the layers of rock far enough to be heated and flow back to the surface. We love those hot springs, enjoying them at the end of a long day. Nearby we find occasional exposure of the old Modoc seabed showing the diatoms of ocean life in pure white earth. Another result of the layers is the existence of lovely rock points from volcanic andesite flaked over thousands of years by native people. As distant in time as those craftsman seem, they were here moments ago compared to the geologic drama of the rocky layers.

The whole story, tectonic plates pushing against each other, mountains rising and then eroding to become sandstone, seabed diatoms found at the top of 5,000 foot peaks: it is more like Greek mythology than history. On some days, I would prefer to believe that mischievous spirits direct the flow from our gray water system to surprising places. Or that disputes among quarreling gods result in smoke and rumbles from volcanic Cascade peaks. When I imagine the complicated layers beneath our quiet pasture, I can almost hear those spirits moving about. On other days, I find the unbelievable time depth of the geologic story comforting. This earth represents a long term commitment to growth and change and diversity.

FOUR CORNERS

In the fall of 1970, I traveled 60 miles into the mountains from Redding with a pair of local newspaper reporters to the site of the Pit River tribal land occupation at Four Corners. The site lies at the intersection of State Highway 299 and State Highway 89, just east of the town of Burney. Four Corners is part of the 3.4 million acres northeast of Redding that constitute the Pit River tribe's ancestral land. The Four Corners site is claimed now by the U.S. Forest Service. More than 100 Indians, including men, women and children, had moved onto this land, cutting trees to make a village site and putting up a Quonset hut in preparation for winter. Among the equipment they had used to level the occupation area was a backhoe and grader owned by the local poverty program where I worked. They had not asked for the equipment explicitly to clear an occupation site, of course, but to grade bad roads in the rural backcountry where houses clustered.

It was a crisp fall day, with the vivid yellows and reds that are a part of this high desert, volcanic plateau area. In the background, the Hat Creek rim of blocky black lava defines the narrow valley through which Highway 89 runs. Vegetation is sparse in this arid country, but ponderosa pine, incense cedar, and Douglas fir dotted the area of the occupation. There is little understory to this forest, in part due to the dry climate east of the Cascade mountains. In addition, the land here is the product of eons of lava flows, resulting in a thin soil over porous basalt that does not hold enough water for shallow-rooting plants. The result is an open park-like forest. Mount Shasta is visible to the northwest, Mount Lassen to the southwest. Fire has shaped this land as well, periodically burning quickly through the forest. The Pit River Indian ancestors regularly set fires to drive game, stimulate growth of seed and berry plants, collect insects, and promote grass for deer. Today, lightning and careless campers do the job.

There was an American flag hanging in a tree, and a large sign inviting other Indians to join the gathering. Two Indian women were cooking venison stew on an outdoor fire, and the carcass of another deer was hanging from a tree limb near the flag. Other women were setting picnic tables with salads, cakes, and coffee. They were, of course, Forest Service tables. Three older men were drumming, and a dozen children were tumbling about. There were battered old pickups parked helter-skelter around the raked dirt site. It smelled of campfire and venison and was welcoming when we arrived.

It was romantic to imagine that the deer had been captured by digging big pitfalls along established game trails. Early settlers in this area named the Pit River and the Pit River Indians for the pits used by Indians for hunting. It seems more likely, however, that modern rifles were involved in the demise of the deer I saw that day. Indeed, I suppose that I had an unconscious expectation that an Indian occupation would be made by people in buckskins. The people assembled were dressed in jeans and t-shirts or flannel shirts, and tennis shoes or well-worn logging boots. Everything from the clothes to the cookware showed the relative poverty of the community, as well as a comfort with living partly outdoors and welcoming large groups. Indeed, a smaller version of this gathering could have taken place in any poor section of the county, including Big Wheels Ranch. The people here looked like who they were: poor, loggers and construction guys, motel maids or quick-stop clerks. The children looked delighted to be out of doors and not in school. Even the headbands and the drumming had been co-opted in enough non-Indian gatherings to seem familiar.

The occupation took place to mark the start of a trial in nearby Burney of ten Indians, who had the previous June taken over a campground claimed by Pacific Gas and Electric (PG&E) in Big

Bend, twenty miles away on the Pit River. The Indians were charged with trespassing. The Indian defense was that the Pit River tribe never signed a treaty for the 3.4 million acres that was their ancestral land. PG&E has built a series of dams on the Pit River and one result is that salmon, historically a mainstay of the Pit River people, no longer move up the river. A proclamation at that first occupation issued by Pit River Tribal Leader Mickey Gemmill stated: "We are the rightful and legal owner of the land. No amount of money can buy the Mother Earth……The Earth is our mother and we cannot sell her."

I was drawn to this conflict in large part by a fascination with the words and spirit of tribal elder Raymond Lego. I had met Raymond as part of my job at the poverty program. Typically dressed in a plaid shirt and jeans, wearing a bead necklace with a bear tooth, Raymond was blocky like many in this tribe, but wiry with a face lined by lots of time outside. He moved quietly and spoke softly. He also had a quiet and strong moral force to his presence. Earlier in the fall he had encouraged me to attend a salmon ceremony outside Redding, where salmon still travelled upstream. Indian men stood in the fast-running stream until their hands and feet were the temperature of the water. The water was freezing cold, almost literally freezing in the crisp early morning. The men then walked up beside the salmon and simply plucked them out of the water. It took my breath away. Raymond had said about the earlier Big Bend occupation that "An Indian is not an Indian if he has no land base…We have been rendered powerless. We have lost our voice. We want to rebuild it."

These occupation efforts had ties to the occupation of Alcatraz Island by the American Indian Movement. The urban multi-tribal mix that occupied Alcatraz focused on the breadth of broken treaties and unrecognized tribal rights. The Pit River tribal occupation was very rural, in a small community where tribal members had gone to school with the law enforcers and worked alongside white timber workers. Land use was driven by Pacific Gas and Electric dam building and by large timber companies. Local law enforcement, the district attorney, and the judiciary in Burney were concerned that the strategies of urban politics might be used in this rural area. Judge Phelps in Burney had already warned the defense lawyers representing the Indians during the earlier occupation that he was not going to let the case become "another Chicago," referring to the publicized trial of the Chicago Seven on conspiracy charges after the Democratic National Convention in 1968. I was so moved by the rhetoric of Raymond, and the injustice of the treatment of these proud people over the last hundred-plus years, that I thought I knew them.

There was wood smoke in the air and the happy shouts of children on a camping adventure. I was welcome because of my connection with the poverty program that had produced the backhoe and grader. My two reporter friends were welcome because of their ability to articulate the purpose of this occupation to a broader community. The tribe, in any event, was eager to welcome private individuals to the discussion and to assure us that their intention was not to disturb individual land-holdings. In this rural area they knew, of course, of my connection with Big Wheels Ranch. Their fight was with the government and the corporations like PG&E that benefitted from the land and from the wealth of its hydropower. There was a metaphor in the erection of this encampment next to the huge power lines that carried that hydropower southwest to urban electric users.

Despite the welcome informed by politics, our white faces made us "others." I joined the women setting out a meal, recognizing Diane whose child was in Head Start and who served on an advisory board to the poverty program. She was a beautiful woman with a fall of shiny black hair and a big grin, but she was also fierce enough to back down her tall, handsome husband despite his tribal leadership position. I tried to feel comfortable, even though tribal members do not engage in the chit-chat of urban folks. In my own mind, I found myself looking at the scene as though it were a movie. Political sympathy on my part did not turn these occupiers into friends. When these folks said 'this land is my land,' it had a resonance that I don't think I fully understood. I was, after all, a white girl thinking of the distant past compared to an Indian reliving a virtual genocide. It took some time for me to recognize the extent to which cultural differences and unshared history created a gulf between us. Moreover, underneath the air of camping, the adults were tense. Diane had the look on her face that she had when she told me in a poverty program meeting that my antiwar attitudes were not shared by her people. Diane's husband, Junior, who was affable when he arranged for the loan of road grading equipment, was stern and distant, looking like the model for a nickel. The rumors that brought the reporters here had reached the occupation site as well. Law enforcement intended to evict the occupiers from what officials believed was Forest Service land.

Fifty-two law enforcement personnel, including federal agents, state troopers, and county sheriffs arrived mid-morning with 50 forest service personnel. This made about as many enforcers as there were occupiers. Law enforcement announced that they were there to arrest people on charges of illegal timber cutting and illegal construction of the hut. A scene that had included conversations and the laughter of children stilled and we all held our breath. Ross Montgomery, another tribal leader, began to cut a cedar tree near the Quonset hut with a chain saw. The officers told him to stop. When he did not, the officers said they would take away his saw. The drummers continued to maintain a slow beat as the situation deteriorated. Most of the women and children moved inside the Quonset hut, not afraid exactly, but protective. Men, from teenagers to elders, massed to defend the tribe and the hut. Mickey Gemmill and Ross Montgomery both restated that they did not want violence, but that every member of the tribe would resist dismantling the occupation. The discussion over the saw failed and a club-swinging confrontation broke out. Some of the women came out from the Quonset hut to help their men and to curse at the officers. Groups of people rolled on the ground. Men and women were sprayed with mace and clubbed. The sheriff said that his officers were attacked with pine clubs. Indians were wrestled or beaten to the ground, handcuffed, and dragged to squad cars.

All of a sudden my movie of valiant Indians defending the Mother Earth had become an immediate and threatening reality. The casual violence of the encounter, on both sides, was way outside the comfort zone created by my urban childhood. The only time I had hit anyone, or been hit, was in childhood squabbles with my four brothers. I thought of myself as a pacifist. I believed that the world would be a better place if we talked together. This violence included law enforcement beatings and mace spraying. It reflected an Indian belief that their land and their culture was dying. I had been in trouble already at the poverty program when I urged a woman member of the Montgomery clan to report domestic abuse over her black eye. She told me to mind my own business: her husband was nursing a broken jaw after the incident. On this fall day I was brought face to face with the distance that my youth and cultural otherness brought to the table. I fled to our car and cried.

When most of the fighting Indians had been subdued, Forest Service workers advanced on the Quonset hut with crowbars and hammers. Women and young men fought in the dark hut to hold them back, in the end fleeing out the back door. Twenty-three Indians were arrested on charges of interfering with law enforcement officers. None were arrested for trespassing, which would have potentially raised in court the question of whose land this was anyway. One of the reporters I traveled with was arrested on charges of interfering with a federal officer, despite (or perhaps because of) being armed only with a reporter's notebook. One of the Indians was hospitalized with injuries after the battle.

There was a strong belief in the Indian community that the violence of this confrontation was historical and predictable. It had to do with more than the enforcement of what was, in their view, bad law. There were persistent rumors of a white supremacist organization in the area. My own experience at the poverty program was the discovery that every single child identified for Special Education in Burney was Pit River Indian. This passive violence against a culture was enforced by white administrators. But I was new to my job. Even though I had met the tribal leadership, these relationships were tentative. Fundamentally, I was not prepared for the violence on display that day. The violence that troubled the Pit River tribe was that done to the river, to the salmon run and to tribal traditions. Their children were treated unfairly in school. This day was part of a nearly 200-year-long clash of values and culture. The violence that troubled me was the prospect of people hitting people. The reality here was more complex and the stakes more grave. So I cried. I cried for my own safety; I cried for my reporter friend's arrest; I cried over the end of a gallant political stand; I cried a little for those salmon. Perhaps I cried at the discovery that violent revolutionary confrontation was not in my nature.

The courts in the end did not ratify the claims of the Pit River tribe. The government's legal argument appeared to be that the federal government could, and did, appropriate land in the 1850's without a treaty and without compensation. Only one of those arrested served any time, and that person was convicted of assault. I spent many hours explaining to the FBI why a grader and backhoe belonging to the poverty program were confiscated at the occupation site. My argument was that when the tribe asked for equipment to prepare roads for the winter, it was my job to provide whatever we had. This was the people's backhoe, after all. It seemed to prevail, although the government held onto the equipment for months and months as the various court cases wound their way through the justice system. Far too many members of the Pit River tribe continue to live in poverty today. Salmon still do not move up the Pit River. A casino and gas station in Burney provide more employment and the funds for better health care and housing. Still, too little has changed. A new version of land occupation is unfolding in the 21st century a couple of hundred miles north of here at the Malheur Wildlife Refuge in Oregon. So-called cowboys occupy federal land in support of beleaguered ranchers. In the course of the occupation, the cowboys drive backhoes through sacred areas, disturbing Indian artifacts. A plea on behalf of a century-old ranching culture appears not to recognize a 10,000 year old land use culture. We haven't made much progress in sharing this land.

THE POVERTY PROGRAM

On October 8, 1971, I found myself part of a sit-in at the local welfare office. More than two dozen women who depended on what was then called Aid to Families with Dependent Children (AFDC) initiated the protest after Governor Ronald Reagan's "welfare reform" tied up the checks they needed to feed their families. With the help of a VISTA volunteer named Mary Ellen, they organized themselves as the Shasta County Welfare Rights Organization (WRO) and invaded the welfare office on that Friday morning to make their case. At this point, their checks were more than a week overdue and they had run out of food. I joined them as part of my new job with the Community Action Program (CAP), which supported their effort.

Three of the original purchasers of Big Wheels Ranch worked at CAP. I went to work at CAP when my husband and I separated, and it was there I met the WRO members. The CAP, or poverty program, was a mixture of young idealists who believed that our work would make a difference for people living in poverty. The wages and working conditions fitted our poverty program name: no one was getting a lot of money in this work. Our offices were in an old machine shop with cement floors; our furniture was surplus from other government programs or simply found items from the local Good Will. Part of our job was to help the people in groups like the Welfare Rights Organization speak for themselves about their needs.

In January 1971, Governor Reagan proposed a state budget that included significant cuts to welfare. In late summer, the Legislature adopted a package of these "reforms," including substantial reductions in the amounts paid to many families. Rules for the reductions arrived in local welfare offices at the beginning of October. The monthly amount of welfare paid to many women and children was going to change; in most cases it would get smaller. We talked at WRO meetings about why the state took nine months to negotiate a "reform" package and expected local welfare departments to implement the changes immediately.

This state-level picture was made more confusing and more dismal by the county welfare department. The County Welfare Director had been in her job for many years. To call her rigid is an understatement. She had helmet hair and thick make-up to match a tight-ass approach to her job. Her main goal was to be sure that no mistakes were made. So, the staff in the welfare department painstakingly calculated and recalculated every check individually after the passage of the new laws. It was taking an agonizingly slow time. The sit-in happened on a Friday, October 8, when the checks were already overdue a week.

A half-dozen of us, including Mary Ellen and I, went to the

welfare office that Friday morning. We did not bring our children. The kids, including my three-year-old Ben, were being cared for by Pete, a plan-writer at the CAP and member of Big Wheels Ranch. Betty, the chair of the Welfare Rights Organization, led our group and would be our main spokesperson. She was enormous, with red hair, bright red lipstick, and a floral print house dress. She was regal, and proved on that day to be graceful under pressure. Her vice-chair was Bobbi, a tiny, dark-haired woman with a shrill voice that she was not shy about using.

We did not go intending to provoke a confrontation, however. We went because the women and their children could not make it through the weekend without getting their checks. The welfare office was a one-story, low-rent office building in downtown Redding. The whole room was gray: cheap gray carpet, cheap gray folding chairs, and smudged gray walls. The windows were dirty and water-spotted. It smelled of strong disinfectant. There was no attempt to make the space welcoming, no toys or children's area, no plants or posters on the wall. There was just a receptionist, dressed in a bright summer dress and wearing the bouffant bubble hairdo that was popular in Redding that year. She sat behind a tall counter to take names and direct people to the rows of chairs to wait for a social worker. No wonder she and the other workers in this office were depressed. But the office was air conditioned on this Indian summer day, so it was better than the CAP office where we normally met.

Betty walked to the counter and asked to speak to the Director. She was not here, the receptionist told us. Well, let us speak to whoever is in charge. The receptionist was already nervous and asked us to sit down. So we walked to the chairs to wait while she called to the back office. There were at least ten other women sitting on those gray chairs, there to ask for their money, overdue for a week now. They, of course, had had to bring their children, who were pinballing around the bleak gray room. All of us, the WRO members and the others, were in our thrift-store best. After all, none of us were trying to scare the staff.

We waited, and we waited. At least an hour passed. Betty went back to the receptionist to ask when we might talk to someone. The receptionist by now had compressed lips and white spots next to her nose. The bored and rowdy children were a trial; the desperate women were embarrassing. It was clear that she wanted us all to know that she was not like us. The Deputy Director will talk to you when he is free, she said. She seemed to imply that we would be at the bottom of any priority list in this office, even if these women were the reason she had a job.

Betty and Bobbi began to explain to the other women that they were part of an organization that gathered together to help poor women survive. Betty said that she, like them, was there to ask that the checks be released before the weekend. Bobbi said angrily that her worthless ex-husband at least paid child support to the county, but that the county was holding even that money. They would not release the child support until they figured out the whole grant amount under the new rules. The county was denying her two children even that small proof that their daddy cared they ate and had a roof over their heads. They explained that Mary Ellen and I – not ourselves on welfare – were there not to speak for them but to support them. Two of the waiting women began to cry, saying that they had already received eviction notices. Three others said they really, truly had no food in the house at all. It seemed that we were indeed all in this together. Betty invited the women to join us in our group request. We hoped that the message that we were all stronger together was powerful for these women. She offered that the children could join ours nearby with Pete. Perhaps the offer of babysitting on a hot and trying day was powerful. Whatever it was, most of the women asked if they could stick with us.

It was at least another hour before the Deputy Director appeared.

During that whole time, none of the women had been called. What on earth were they doing behind those closed doors in back of the receptionist? The Deputy was overweight, and tidy in his slacks and tie. He had thick glasses and slicked-back black hair and a bald spot he was trying to cover with a bad comb-over. This room full of desperate women scared him. The Director was out of town. (At least the Deputy said she was out of town.) He pleaded that he would be glad to make an appointment with the Director for next week. It was clear over the course of the day that he was working above his competence level.

Betty made our fundamental demand: that checks be given immediately to these families that depended on the money for food and shelter. It wasn't much: the most that any family of three received at this time was $235, less than $60 per week. How could anyone live on that, much less live without it?

The Deputy said that he did not have the authority to release checks. Another woman explained, calmly at first, that she and others in the group didn't live in the kinds of places where the landlord would wait until the Welfare Director came back to town and double-checked that all the check amounts were correct. Bobbi explained, or rather shrieked, that the county was holding the child support paid by her children's father; they could at least release the money that wasn't theirs. The Deputy explained that the county had to hold all funds until the exact size of each family's check was decided at the state and local office. At this point, the frustrated women began to talk over each other. "How do we pay the rent?" "What do we feed our kids?" The workers in this office knew that no husbands or dads to the children were at home to help.

In fact, social workers regularly checked for shoes under the bed, since no mother could get welfare if she was living with a man. The Deputy Director said over and over again that he could not give out checks. He could not take any action without the Director's OK, and she was, as he already told us, out of town.

As the day wore on, it became harder and harder to remain calm. What part of the problems created by no check didn't they understand? We rounded up the children from those women newly recruited to the WRO, and any others who were simply too desperate to leave without a check. We walked them over to a nearby corner park to join Pete, who had rustled up a picnic lunch and did not seem dismayed at the growing day camp.

By mid-afternoon, the sit-in mood shifted again. Even with the air conditioning, both our group and the office staff were hot and sweaty. The smell of old clothes, too many people in a small space, the remnant smells of children who had fussed and run and bounced around with nothing to do, began to overwhelm the smell of disinfectant. You could smell the stress and fear, from desperate women with hungry children and from staff who didn't know what would happen next. The Deputy Director, his crisp shirt now wilting and his tie askew, sweat showing under his arms, asked us all to leave. He was not ugly with us, but he had his marching orders from his boss and they did not include issuing checks.

At this point, each side called in some outside troops. We called in lawyers and preachers. The welfare office called in lawyers and guys with guns. Local Reverend George Lindsay, from Pilgrim Congregational Church arrived on our side. Tall and skinny with large bright blue eyes, he worked often with the poverty program and made his church available for our board meetings. In his gentle way, he offered to mediate a discussion between the WRO leadership and the welfare department. He said, "let's talk about a solution for these women and children." The Deputy Director said he had no authority to mediate and called in a lawyer from the County Counsel's office. The Counsel told the deputy director that the office was not required to deliver checks on this day, and recommended that he not negotiate with us.

We called Mary Ellen's husband, an attorney with the Legal Services program of the CAP. He told us that he was working with a local judge to get an injunction to force the welfare department to release checks, but it was unlikely that such an injunction would work in one afternoon.

Meanwhile, everyone became more anxious, sweaty and angry. Desperate women were being asked to be patient by middle-class office workers whose salary checks, from the same welfare budget, had arrived on time at the first of the month. At this point, the welfare department called in their ultimate weapon. A police sergeant, as sweaty and uncomfortable as the rest of us, arrived to tell us that we were trespassing if we stayed after we were asked to leave. He begged us to leave, saying he didn't want to arrest anyone. Mei-ling, an experienced WRO member and mother of two young children, was as direct as always. She said, "Why wouldn't we go to jail? At least we'd have food and shelter."

At just about 6 p.m., the police issued the last warning and then led 16 of us to the paddy wagon. We linked arms and sang "Battle Hymn of the Republic" and "Onward Christian Soldiers." (What else would we all know the words to?) The paddy wagon was dark inside and smelled like all the unhappy people who had travelled this same road. Up until then, it had all been exhilarating, a chance to make a stand, an opportunity to call out bureaucratic bumbling, or viciousness. (Really? You won't talk to us?) Our children, about 20 of them, were all together, being cared for by Uncle Pete.

I had not been an activist before this, except in a distant, letter-writing sort of way. I had food and shelter at my house. But I was recently separated from my husband, who thought that it was only sexism in the courts that resulted in my having custody of our 3-year-old, since he was the responsible citizen and I was the rowdy, hippie flake. Could I lose custody because of this day's arrest? So, I was the one crying in a huddle on the floor of the paddy wagon, being comforted by women who truly did not know where their next meal or rent payment was coming from.

The paddy wagon, though only travelling a few blocks to the jail, jounced over every pothole as if the driver was aiming for the roughest possible ride in this aging vehicle with, apparently, no springs at all. Then Bobbi, who thought of herself as the fearless one among us, completely lost it in the claustrophobic, bouncy wagon and began screaming. She also was hugged and comforted by Betty, who murmured over and over, "We are all together here; we can get through this." Mary Ellen, another woman with food and shelter at home, had her own moment of truth when the police brought the garage gate down with a clang behind the paddy wagon at the jail. It rang like the sound track of every prison movie we had ever seen. Wavering a bit in her red, white and blue outfit, she reached through the gate to squeeze the hand of her husband Archie. He assured us that the CAP team would get us out of there.

When we got to the county jail, the dynamic changed again. The jail prisoners, mostly men, had learned that 16 women, mostly young, were arriving in a paddy wagon. They began banging on the bars, leaning out into the corridors, offering all kinds of welcome to these new prisoners, in a truly astonishing din. Their yelling should have been at least a little threatening, but in an odd way it felt more like they were joining our challenge. They were, after all, already behind bars. So we continued to sing. Then Pete arrived outside with all the children, including my adorable 3-year-old Ben. I had imagined they would be frightened, but they weren't. They had had a picnic with Uncle Pete. Then they spent the afternoon on an art project, making picket signs that said, "Let my Mommy go." Then they got to have a parade. They began marching around the jail and chanting. Finally, the Reverend Lindsay arrived along with the Reverend John Albright from the Methodist Church, who also served as the CAP Board chair. The two men of the cloth offered to guarantee bail.

On that night, only a handful of the protesters were booked and released; the rest, including me, were issued citations and we all went home. The checks were not released on that Friday, although they did arrive the next week. We leveraged food through the CAP and with the assistance of local church groups so that children did not go hungry. The Legal Services office worked with landlords to assure that families did not lose their homes. The District Attorney dropped the charges later, so none of us wound up with a record. In the end, we did not reverse the long, relentless reduction in aid and support for poor women initiated by Ronald Reagan. We probably did not even convince a majority of the county residents that we are all in this together and that hungry mothers and children living in unstable situations are a shame and a danger to us all.

By 1971, the poverty program nationwide was no longer new. The enthusiasm of the mid-1960's for ending poverty was fading. The financial support promised by President Lyndon Johnson when he established the program was disappearing into the growing defense budget in support of the war in Vietnam. Ronald Reagan was Governor of California, and he initiated various attacks on local programs. A part of the motivation for some living at Big Wheels was to achieve a sense of safety in a hostile political environment for those of us working in the poverty field. The support of friends who could stand together, the knowledge that there was a place of trees and water and welcome to flee to – the ranch provided a sense of sanctuary for me, allowing me to learn this new job.

Many years later, I went to a musical evening and ran into Mei-Ling's two children, now grown and in their 40's. I learned that Mei-Ling went on to earn a nursing certification and sent her two children through college. There are those who would say that perhaps the reductions to welfare grants propelled families to greater efforts to be self-sufficient, but that was not my experience working at the CAP. Stable housing, enough food to eat, and the community support necessary to identify a goal and the path to achieve it were much likelier to result in a happy outcome. In the final analysis, we all learned a lesson that day in 1971. We were strong and we could stand up to power. We gave all the children a vision of strength and unity, mine included. We activated a community of activists, lawyers, and churches to continue the work. It was good.

VIETNAM

The War in Vietnam is one of the defining political challenges for my generation. For many, the effects of the war were personal and sad. My beloved cousin Kenny died in Vietnam. Tall and handsome, he was my age-mate in a family where all the other cousins were older. We played, told secrets, and hid from view at family reunions and picnics my whole life. One of my earliest memories is the family reunion where I discovered that his mother would allow him to eat white bread with butter and white sugar on it and the crusts cut off. I don't remember what part of this was most shocking, but I was pretty sure that you wouldn't get to heaven if you didn't eat your bread crusts.

Kenny stepped on a grenade in Vietnam. It was early in the war, 1967. My oldest brother was serving a second tour of duty in Vietnam. The army sent him home with Kenny's casket a couple of months early, in an act of family support. Growing numbers of casualties made such individual arrangements impossible later in the war. I was visibly pregnant with my first child at Kenny's funeral. My aunt, Kenny's mother, was devastated by the death of her only son. She sobbed that it just wasn't fair that my mother, who had four sons, was able to see her oldest son home early because of Kenny's death. The exchange permanently altered her relationship with my mother.

As a result of my anti-war activism, my relationship with my mother and both of the brothers who served in the war were affected for years. I returned to the north state from Thanksgiving in Southern California in the early 1970s determined not to struggle through another birth family holiday. Two of my brothers, two and six years younger than I, had served in Vietnam. My mother believed, along with a substantial portion of Americans, that anti-war activities made our soldiers less safe. At the very least, she believed the antiwar movement disrespected military service. Thanksgiving dinner was once again ruined by anger on the part of my mother and suggestions by one brother that perhaps his security clearance was threatened by my activities. Hah! Given how mild my own activities were, it is difficult in retrospect to see them as a threat, or even as effective. For several years thereafter, Thanksgiving would happen at the ranch instead of with my own family.

Similar to my own, virtually every family in the U.S. was affected by the war. More than 3 million Americans served in Vietnam; 58,000 died there; three times that many were wounded. The draft affected decision-making for every young man who came of age in the 1960s or early 1970s. My oldest son, Ben, owes the timing of his birth to the fact that his daddy was graduating from law school, while still eligible for the draft. Fatherhood would ensure that he didn't spend the first years of his career in Saigon.

Others were not avoiding service, but saw it as an opportunity. My first job upon arriving in Northern California was teaching reading at a Job Corps program. The young men in my class were a committed and attentive bunch. Each of them had tried first to enlist in the army, only to discover that the ability to read was required. Army enlistment was their ticket out of poverty, and so they enrolled in the Job Corps hoping to gain the skills to be accepted in the army. It is no coincidence that they were overwhelmingly young men of color. I was pregnant when I taught, and these young men watched as the time for birth drew closer. Among my first sights after Ben was born was the circle of work-dirty young black men, fresh from the site where they were learning construction skills, standing around to admire the brand new baby who was going to keep his Daddy out of the war.

Two years later, I went to work for the local Community Action Program (CAP). By the early 1970s, it was clear that the war in Vietnam would be ending soon. It took somewhat longer for the huge stream of equipment and weaponry from the defense industry to be turned off. One solution was for the federal government to make Department of Defense equipment available to community action programs. Early in the war, we could examine lists of used items that might be helpful: office furniture, used vehicles, barracks furniture, house repair items. Later in the war, brand new equipment, some of which had not even been shipped to Vietnam and back, was available. Trucks, graders, backhoes could be had for the cost of picking up from a military base. There were rumors that we might even be able to snag a helicopter if we had anyone who could fly one.

As a young city girl, my learning curve about all this equipment was pretty steep. On one memorable occasion, I sent a couple of employees down to McClellan Air Force Base three hours away to pick up some wooden doors, described as suitable for our housing rehabilitation program. They were parolees, released from prison where they had served time for white collar crimes. They were assigned as part of their parole to work at the CAP. They were glad to be out of prison, although inclined to turn to a con first when an opportunity presented itself. They were bemused at being supervised by a younger girl with so little experience, and it took all my energy to appear to be the badass required to keep them in line. When the pair had been gone for hours, the phone rang and I identified myself as the supervisor of the equipment unit. There was a long pause. A gruff military voice then said, "I shoulda figured it would be a broad. Listen up because I'm only gonna say this once. You tell those yahoos to bring back my airplane doors before the end of the day. I have the planes to strafe your building." My yahoos were unable to explain how it was that they mistook airplane doors for wooden housing doors. It probably says something about the quality of training we were able to provide. We returned the doors, McClellan did not strafe our building, and we decided to forego the wooden doors from the base.

By the early 1970s, several things were clear. A first-world army was being slowly outmatched by the passion and commitment of a ragtag army of people defending their homes and fighting a civil war. In addition, it appeared that the U.S. was complicit in widespread corruption. Our ally, the South Vietnamese government, was corrupt and heavy-handed, fueling the insurgency among its people. Worse, drugs were awash throughout our armed forces. Even as early as the 1970s, well-substantiated rumors charged that our own government was using drug shipments to finance some activities and to destabilize Southeast Asia. Equipment, medicine and supplies were rumored to be sidetracked and sold on the black market. For our parents, who had experienced World War II, the cynicism of the generation that fought in Vietnam and that protested against our being there was outrageous. For people my age, Vietnam tarnished the clear idealism of Kennedy's call to Camelot, the moral clarity of the Civil Rights movement, the optimism of the War on Poverty. More immediately for me, funding for the war on poverty was significantly diminished by the costs of the war. Our children, born during or immediately after the war, have experienced the impact of the war as well. The war years produced cynicism about politics and a tattered social contract. We are reliving those strains still as the U.S. fights dubious and troubling wars in the Middle East.

Early effects of the war at the ranch were muted. Most of the original ranch purchasers were white college graduates. The war was, for the most part, fought by the sons of blue collar and poor America, by the children of loggers and auto mechanics and single mothers waitressing in diners. However, each of the ranch members was affected by the war, as my family demonstrated. The choice to live at the ranch was surely informed by that reality. The beauty of this particular place, the commitment to a life less driven by consumerism, the sense of refuge from difficult political challenges all played a role.

Most ranch residents worked in town, engaging in work and struggle of various kinds. Before long, however, Vietnam brought a new sensibility to our lives. For a couple of younger residents, service in the armed forces had brought pain. Fred arrived having spent a tour of duty unloading body bags in Vacaville. He was emotionally wounded by the experience. He was seeking healing, not the civic engagement that occupied others. Younger residents who had not served were still cynical about the possibilities for change in any arena, especially through political action. Drugs were more readily available. The tenor of life changed at the ranch, as elsewhere in the U.S.

At the start of the new century, the angst and divisions of the Vietnam war years returned. Members of the ranch, along with like-minded community members, reserved the local community hall to show a documentary about the new US war in Afghanistan. The film was of the left, critical of the reasoning of the Bush adminis-tration, and underscored the long history of colonial war efforts in that part of the world, generally bloody and unsuccessful. I was tasked to emcee the evening, including prompting a discussion. Roughly 30 souls came out to see the movie, all but two of them familiar friends, part of the small but valiant band of lefties in this generally conservative neighborhood.

The two strangers to me were an older couple. They told me that they were excited to see a movie advertised as being about

Afghanistan because their grandson, in the army, was due to leave in a few days to serve there. They knew nothing about the country and were glad to be able to get a look. I told them that this was not a historical work or a travelogue, but was political and would not likely meet their expectations. They determined to stay, and did until the end. Worse was to come. The discussion featured a rowdy attack by audience members on the political decisions that were leading us into "another Vietnam." When our new couple ventured the opinion that 9/11 demanded our response, one rude and aggressive individual attacked them as naïve and reactionary. They left.

A very few weeks later, the local newspaper published the sad news. Our couple's grandson was killed by a roadside bomb within weeks of arriving to the war. We made a belated and rather lame effort to make up for our sin of not respecting their situation and their vulnerability. We donated monthly to a fund established by local veterans that sent care packages regularly to local service members serving in Iraq or Afghanistan.

It should not be surprising that the social divisions generated by the war in Vietnam remain vivid for so many: college-educated folks who fought the decision to engage in the war, blue-collar folks who fought in the war or whose children fought in the war, and family members affected by the war, no matter how they approached it politically. There was grace, perhaps, in the response of the proud Marine veteran who arranged our donation to serving service people. When I told him, in an effort at full disclosure, that we were a group of antiwar folks who nonetheless supported individuals serving their country, he remarked that no one was as antiwar as the guy who had fought in one.

COURTSHIP AND MARRIAGE

The poverty program brought a tall, lanky Southerner into my life, along with organizing and a work life of commitment to social justice. Bill joined the Community Action Program (CAP) to strengthen education for poor people in the area. Bill was aggressive about his heritage as a redneck at the time. He preserved his South Carolinian accent and he wore a red bandanna headband around his shoulder length hair. His idea of a big Saturday night was to fill a jug with equal parts orange juice and Ripple wine and to head to the local pizza parlor to dance. The jug was for hydration in the parking lot in between sets. My mother thought I had lost my mind instead of my heart.

When we began to date, I was living in that cheap apartment building with then three-year-old Ben. It is a measure of local politics and my life on the edges of those politics that my landlord complained. Bill picked me up for a day at the lake with his pickup truck full of multi-colored children from the CAP afterschool program. The truck itself was an old and dented telephone company truck that the kids had painted rainbow colors. The landlord said, "I never said nuthin' when you were goin' out with the nigger, but the redneck with the telephone company truck has got to go." I told him that my mother no longer told me who to date and that I was damned if my landlord was going to start. I began to plan to move.

Saturday night was one thing, but the real courtship was around community organizing. The local Head Start program was operated by the County Superintendent of Schools, not directly by the CAP. Despite national rules assuring that full parent participation in the design of the program was fundamental to the educational objectives of Head Start, the local Superintendent swore that no arrangement where poor women told him what to do was going to stand. Bill and I spent a school year talking to parent groups, officially and unofficially, about whether they were satisfied with the preschool education they were getting through Head Start. Many parents were frightened at the possibility that taking on the local power structure would have long term consequences. Their children, after all, would leave Head Start and go to public elementary school. All the parents, however, knew that disrespect of their families by the school system would be understood by their children. Any doubt that each parent loved her child and had hopes for a brighter future would be harmful. And most were intrigued by the challenge of Head Start: do you mean that parents would be consulted in the hiring of teachers? In the development of curriculum? Even in the nutrition program? Bill and I put hundreds of miles on that old pickup truck, talking and listening and, ultimately, organizing elections at each of the seven Head Start classrooms. At the end of the project, parents voted to revoke management of Head Start by the County Superintendent and ask the CAP to manage the program directly. The national Head Start rules made that decision final. Bill, whose salary at the CAP was partially paid for with a grant from the Superintendent, was let go. I became the Head Start Director.

The clincher for me in the courtship was my son Ben. Bill was the only man I dated who formed a relationship directly with Ben instead of complimenting me on my smart and handsome son. As the courtship progressed, Ben's relationship with Bill was significant in bringing my mother some comfort. Anyone her first grandson loved couldn't be as crazy as he looked. Then, of course, there was the landlord problem. It really was time for me to leave my apartment. Bill offered the spare room in his house with no strings attached (yes, I mean those kind of strings), and Ben and I moved in. Bill was at the time visiting his family in the south, so I had a little time before we tried to figure out if we could live together. I must admit that the spare room part didn't survive the first 24 hours of Bill's return.

Those first few weeks were a signal of the terms of our relationship, however. While in the south, Bill visited his brother who was serving a medical internship in a mental hospital. One of his brother's patients was a young southerner, recently returned from Vietnam, who was ready to be released. Bill told him he was always welcome in northern California. This poor broken young man called me at Bill's house every day to tell me how much progress he had made hitchhiking across the country. It turned out that Bill's 60s-era conviction that mental illness could always be resolved with acceptance and family was optimistic for Bootlegger Mike, as we called him. He was beautiful, sweet, and had fried a significant portion of his brain cells with the drugs he took in Vietnam. He couldn't work and had a hard time remembering any of our names. He usually called me Mom. Before he wandered off a year later, in lieu of rent he painted much of the house with bold colors and left behind a canvas with an otherworldly but cheerful alternative landscape. Bootlegger Mike was the first of many strays that Bill was to bring into my life over the years. Most of them, like Mike, had a basic sweetness that overrode other failings.

As a final footnote, it is worth noting that in the summer I moved into Bill's house I also served as a delegate to the national Democratic Presidential Convention in Miami. I had worked as a volunteer for the Democratic Party in California while married to my first husband. I had spent most of the last year of my marriage working as a paid employee for an anti-war candidate for the U.S. Senate, George Brown. He narrowly lost the primary, and I returned to live for a few more months with my first husband. The campaign for George McGovern brought the wing of the party where I had worked to the forefront in California. When McGovern won the California primary, I was selected as a 'super-delegate' to attend the convention. The selection, I should say, was less about special things I brought to the election and more about the lack of big donors or party leaders in our part of the north state. John Burton, a California Congressman at the time, co-chaired the delegation with Assembly Member Willie Brown and United Farm Worker leader Dolores Huerta. When John called to offer me the delegate slot, he said, "This could be the only time our wing of the party controls the delegation. You have to come along to Miami." I raised the money from friends and supporters and flew to Miami.

It was an exhilarating experience. The first couple of days were taken up with complicated back room wrangles over whether to seat various delegations. Alternative delegations from Mississippi and Illinois challenged the historic Democratic machine for seats. The traditional Democratic party in California challenged the winner-take-all rules that governed our delegation's membership at the time. While delegates like me in the disputed delegations hung around waiting for the Rules Committee to rule on the challenges so we could be formally seated, the national press corps also hung around waiting for the convention to begin. At this moment, I received a phone call at the convention center. In those pre-cell-phone days, this was remarkable. I flew to an actual phone booth, terrified that something had happened to son Ben. It was the Shasta County Counsel, telling me that the county believed that my attendance as a delegate made me an elected official, and that the formal seating as a delegate would be a violation of the federal Hatch Act, which governed political activities by elected officials. If I did not return home immediately, before I was seated as a delegate, I would be fired from my job at the CAP. It is a measure of my youth and political optimism that I actually told him I couldn't leave. "We are making the revolution here in Miami." Given the fact that McGovern, nominated later that week, only carried one state and the District of Columbia, my faith seems endearing today. I should also add that McGovern carried six counties in California, and that three of them were in our north state area. Our work resulted in success in half of the counties carried by McGovern! I might have been naïve, but along with Bill and other local Democrats, we could organize.

I immediately called Bill in a panic. He said not to worry. Between his unemployment and my child support, we could live just fine. That sealed the deal for me on living together; I wanted that optimism and commitment in my life, even if it meant sharing that life with Bootlegger Mike and various other folks. What happened next was equally exciting. As I left that phone booth, I literally ran into George Moscone, then in the State Senate. He said I looked awful and asked what had happened. When I told him, he put his arm around me. "Let me be your lawyer, at least until we get back to California. You and I will make beautiful press conferences together." And indeed, we had a brief few hours of fame in front of a bored national press corps. As we walked into our first press meeting, George warned me. "Don't talk. When I start describing this single parent country woman, struggling to support her son, bullied by the conservative forces of officialdom, try to let a tear trickle down your cheek. If you talk, you'll blow the description." It must have worked, because my mother in Southern California saw the news and was in a panic. My brother, in the army, swore that I had jeopardized his security clearance.

The rest of that story played out over nearly two years. The CAP was forced to rehire me, pending the outcome of a hearing before the U.S. Civil Service Commission. Challenges to the Hatch Act by a postal workers union, claiming that the Act violated our rights to free speech, resulted in the court affirming the Act. This meant that my case had no precedent-setting value. George handed my defense over to the ACLU and my case was joined to that of a woman from Monterey County named Pearl, who had been fired from her California Employment Development Department job. More to the point, Watergate also happened. By the time we had our hearing before a Civil Service Commission administrative law judge, it was clear that the very last thing the federal government wanted to do was fire a black state worker in her fifties and a white country woman, by now visibly pregnant. It was also clear that we had violated the Hatch Act by acting as delegates while working in jobs supported by federal funds. The judge pleaded with us: "If your supervisor granted you permission, if you even thought that the supervisor's body language gave you permission, your guilt may not be clear." I was pregnant, tired of the hassle and the uncertainty. I was on the verge of saying, "That's it, that's what happened." Pearl stood up to respond: "Your people brought my people here two hundred years ago in chains in the holds of ships. Today you are denying me the right to participate in the democratic process." I said: "I came with her; I'm leaving with her." The judge said we would hear soon. A guilty verdict would mean being fired from the CAP, where I now directed the Head Start program, and a bar against any federal or federally supported employment for seven years. We waited and waited and waited. My ACLU lawyer called, just weeks, it turned out, before Nixon's resignation. The Civil Service Commission lawyer said that my file seemed to have disappeared, perhaps fallen behind the filing cabinet.

And so, we married, prompted by my pregnancy. We had a very low key wedding, Bill in blue jeans and bandanna, me in my very best long patchwork skirt. We were joined by two good friends and Democratic organizing colleagues who brought the beer. The local Superior Court Judge, also a friend, bicycled over to sign the official paperwork. Ben, then five, pronounced the words of the ceremony: "Bill, do you take this mother to be your wife? Do you want to see my magic trick?" So it was done.

In addition to organizing, much of our courtship and the early years of our marriage took place in and around the ranch. It had become the second home that it was to remain throughout our work lives. The ranch was also the location where Bill presented me with what amounted to my engagement present. I had had an unfortunate fight over pigs with my first husband. Bill was eager to prove that, unlike his predecessor, he was a fan of pigs. He drove to ranch country east of our place, on a foggy and rainy day, and negotiated with a rancher over the purchase of a couple of young pigs. In retrospect, that rancher likely saw a willing but inexperienced buyer coming. Bill pointed out a couple in the field but did not double-check when the farmer loaded the pigs into the back of the pickup. When he arrived back at the ranch to proudly present them to me, they were skinny little things with long, stilt-like legs. Nevertheless, we penned them at the ranch, got advice on how to feed them, and watched them grow into taller, skinny pigs with very long legs. At one point, we moved them to the hippie preschool in Redding where Ben attended, to be fed and admired by the children. We kept them past the first year, which is the maximum time for slaughter, and determined that we would breed these two female pigs. We took them to the farm of our pig consultant on the outskirts of Redding. He kept them through two fertility cycles and then called with the bad news. "Each time they came into season, I would send the boar into their pen and they just beat the crap out of him. I believe that you have found two lesbian pigs." When we finally did slaughter the pigs, we figured that it was the most expensive pork we had ever eaten. We savored every part of the pig except that I wimped out on the preparation of head cheese and gave the head to one of the Head Start parents.

We did make one other connection with those pigs. We slaughtered them in 1974. At the time, George Moscone was running for Governor. I put together a series of campaign events and photo opportunities in the Redding area as a part of a road tour he did announcing his candidacy. As a part of the day, he came to Ben's preschool. Ben, blond and curly haired, smiled up at George, reached for his hand, and said, "Do you want to come see our pigs?" George, dressed in a lovely and expensive suit with Italian loafers, gamely slithered down the muddy hill in the rain, followed by cameras clicking. Ben filled a can with pig feed and took George in to offer the feed. While he bent over, Mama Nerf came up behind him and put her muddy mouth on the seat of his very expensive pants. George could not shout at me while the cameras were running, but he mouthed, "You owe me for this." To the press he said about those expensive pants, "Perhaps she recognized a relative." When I took him a ham from Mama Nerf, he said only, "I believe I am entitled to this."

We spent much time, with Ben and then baby Bayliss, at the ranch in the early days of our marriage. We hiked the path behind the pasture to the pond at Earth Camp and the spectacular view of Mt. Shasta to the north. We had complicated and extravagant Easter egg hunts, with scavenger hints to follow as the children got older. We snowshoed on the Hatchet pass. We gathered for wood cutting expeditions in the fall to provide a winter's supply of fuel for the wood stoves. We made vats of soup for big family weekend meals. We learned to slaughter the turkey for Thanksgiving. The ranch was a place to become a family, for vacation time, and a refuge during trying political times.

JEFFERSON

I have spent my adult life working on issues of poverty, children and families, and health. Most of my friends and I worked in politics or government or the non-profit world. I spent a central part of my career as a (gasp) lobbyist, albeit for public mental health systems. My mother early on requested that I be discrete about announcing what I really did for a living. "I work in government" was bad enough, without admitting either that I lobbied state legislators, even worked for them politically sometimes, or worked with programs for people who were poor and/or sick. She once told me that I would need a coffin specially built so that my left knee could jerk into eternity.

Imagine the culture shock when I moved full time to the ranch upon my retirement. We are, to say the least, located in the red state part of blue California. Even by red state definitions, this part of the world has a history of efforts to disengage from all things coastal, or modestly liberal, or even Democratic party-aligned. I was fooled by thirty years of visits here to neighbors and friends, not fully realizing that they represent an island in the midst of a larger sea of conservatism.

Early on after our move, a public struggle over the construction of a new energy transmission line through our community presented me with a vivid learning experience about local politics. The proposal was made by a collaborative of publicly-owned utilities and a public meeting was held in the local community center. More than 150 people attended, from a scattered area that has a hard time drawing half that number for cultural events. The meeting was organized by opponents to the project and there was no pretext of fairness or equal time. The remarkable experience for me was the amount of passion, anger and paranoia that emerged. The proposal from the utility company was to bring energy from solar and wind development from areas to our east and transport that energy to urban areas to our south and west.

I started the meeting generally believing that any encouragement to alternative energy sources was a good idea. I soon found that the local opponents were suspicious: "That's ridiculous: land east of here is unsuited for wind or solar." (A note on this: the deserts of Nevada and Utah are east of here.) "Once approved, the utility companies will bring in energy from coal-fired plants to our east; they will use the power lines to justify building new nuclear plants east of here."

I found other arguments somewhat more persuasive. The transmission lines would have no immediate benefit to local residents, as the local power is provided by for-profit Pacific Gas and Electric, not the public power companies who serve valley communities and who proposed to build the power line. There was a belief that property values might well fall and eminent domain be used in return for prices that would surely not be fair. Besides, the local community has already given to the cause, since transmission lines already run from hydropower dams on the Pit River to urban areas north and south of us.

As the evening lengthened, the discussion grew more unhinged. It is true that the science is mixed on the effect of living near energy lines. But at this meeting, individuals asserted that power lines would increase leukemia, cancers, Alzheimer's disease, asthma, heart and lung disease, depression, suicides, allergies.....whew! These effects would only worsen the physical and emotional ills that were caused by government-sponsored weather experiments using airplane contrails. Others believed that power lines made lightning strikes more likely. Given that power lines have been associated with fire, any increase in risk in this neighborhood is alarming, but lightning? The final straw for me was the young, libertarian firebrand who asserted that an additional power line in our neighborhood would make the community a prime target for a stinger missile, IED or other terrorist device. These assertions, each wilder than the last, received wild clapping from the audience. I was glad to have Bill with me, he who was a veteran of even wilder Ku Klux Klan rallies in the deep south in the 1960's. His advice to me: "Always clap at the Klan rally if you want to make it out safely."

It is easy to make fun of paranoia expressed in the heat of discussion. Concerns about fire and the impact on neighbors of public utilities are real and should be addressed with the best science we can find. Maybe it is also fair to complain that our area has already given to the cause, and that it is time for folks in urban and suburban areas to step up. When windmills are installed off the coast of Marin County, perhaps we'd be more interested in another sacrifice of land and viewshed. The alarming realization for me at this meeting was the extent of paranoia, anger, and fear in my neighbors. Many of these folks are concerned about global warming. They do believe that it falls to each of us to respond to the threat of climate change. But they, like so many others in the U.S., also believe that government no longer represents collective action. Instead, it is run by some outside group of 'bureaucrats', in a decision-making framework we cannot influence. Is there really no fundamental difference between a corporate decision-making entity like Pacific Gas and Electric and publicly owned utilities or local government land use planners? The take-to-the-streets anger and full-throated yelling of talk radio and much of cable television has convinced many that civility is for chumps.

The signature evidence of these local politics is a movement to establish our county as part of a State of Jefferson. This effort originated as a chamber of commerce project rather than a political movement. In the 1930s, merchants in southern Oregon were joined by merchants in far northern California to protest the failure of Legislatures in both states to build the railroads and highways that would allow business to flourish. A flag was developed, with a centerpiece of two X's, to symbolize the double-cross by the two states. A somewhat lighthearted effort to establish a border gate in northern California was picked up by urban media, probably as evidence of "those amusing rustics." The stated goal of the movement was the establishment of a separate state that could act on behalf of these rural parts of both states; the actual goal seems likely to have been a response by the state governments to local commercial needs. The movement ended abruptly with the start of World War II.

Today, the highways leading to our part of the world have large signs announcing your arrival in Jefferson and the new-state movement is resurgent. Several California counties have adopted resolutions supporting the withdrawal of counties from California and Oregon to establish a new state (although not our county of Shasta). There is, of course, some rural reality to the complaints of some in the potential State of Jefferson. Poverty rates are high in these rural areas, and unemployment more common than in urban areas. The infrastructure of roads, internet service, and cell service is often spotty or absent. However, the Jefferson folks have an edgy and angry agenda. Supporters want a return to unfettered logging, free of environmental requirements such as streamside protection and endangered species protection. Supporters want unfettered ranching, with an end to such outrages as grazing fees on public lands. Supporters want a return of good mining jobs, including the freedom to mine for minerals on public lands. In general, they want much, much smaller government and an end to burdensome federal and state regulations. The claim is that an end to regulations would magically free up millions in tax dollars that could be returned to honest tax-paying citizens. To a large extent, this claim is belied by the simple fact that the north state is a net tax recipient, with the money for public schools, welfare and health plans, public lands, resources and park staff and administrators, state fire fighters and other public expenditures exceeding the amount that this economically depressed area contributes.

This is a well-armed part of the state. In light of nearby militia activity, an aura of threat can hang over State of Jefferson rallies. This is also a mostly white movement. The anger of poverty and limited expectations, poor health care and low education, so visible in national politics in 2015 is often on view in our part of the world as well. What am I to do, except keep my public sector retirement payments a secret and clap at those rallies?

Chapter 2
Growing Family

*Perhaps the greatest gift of ceremony is its potential to gather
together all the parts of a life*

Teresa Jordan, *Riding the White Horse Home*

Commons: A common, or commons, is land that belongs to an entire community. More specifically, it is open land held in common by the people of a town for shared pasturage or the gathering of firewood. As noted in 'A Gazetteer of Illinois' in 1834 by J.M. Peck, 'A common is a tract of land…in which each owner of a village lot has a common but not an individual right…" —Donna Seaman

Barry Lopez, Ed, *Home Ground: Language for an American Landscape*

We have always called Big Wheels Ranch a commune. That word conjures an exotic list of possibilities. Some communes in the 1960s and 70s were the product of a counterculture movement, embracing anarchy, sex, drugs, and rock and roll. Some communes were, and are, the product of a single, charismatic figure, or small group of figures, and can be cults. Some require purposeful or intentional commitments, such as a shared philosophy or common purpose. Some communes attempt self-sufficiency, and some are driven by a presumed need to survive a coming catastrophe. Some living arrangements that look communal are in fact family arrangements, where families of several generations and varying degrees of relatedness live together.

Big Wheels Ranch, at the beginning, consisted of a group of people who worked together and who wanted a beautiful piece of land that none of the group could afford, or manage, individually. None of the motives for a 'commune' outlined above were articulated. Two couples and three single people were a part of the group. Most worked together in the local poverty program. Others were friends. They might be said to share some common philosophy, but commitment to that philosophy was not a precondition to joining the group. It is probably important that the name for the enterprise came not from a philosophical or political reference but from the existence at the entrance to the property of two very large, iron-rimmed wooden wheels used to haul logs from the woods almost 100 years ago.

The ranch was not, however, separate and distinct from the life and times of the early 1970s. Early on, several younger people joined the ranch in addition to the original purchasers, for varying periods of time. Sex and rock and roll were a part of those times, and drugs, at least of the mild kind, made an appearance as well. Some harbored dreams of living off the land in a return to simpler times. Others fled a life dominated by an unpopular and unsuccessful war of colonialism. Some fled urban unrest that included riots and assassinations. All who arrived were dismayed at the consumerism that characterized life for many Americans. Each of these motivations survives at the ranch today. None of them are adequate on their own to describe what holds us together.

I visited and enjoyed the ranch from the earliest days, as the original purchasers were poverty program colleagues and women's movement sisters. Shortly after Bill and I married in 1973, we purchased a share in the ranch. We did not live there initially, and soon moved to Sacramento for work. Throughout the thirty years that followed, we spent some weekends and vacations at the ranch with our children. We participated in the meetings and debates that shared ownership requires. We participated in work weekends, to repair houses, cut firewood, maintain irrigation lines. As retirement neared, we determined that it was time, perhaps past time, to live at the ranch. We have been residents now for over a decade.

CARRIE NATION RISES

I huffed the backpack onto a log at the trailhead and gingerly slid into it, tightening the waist and shoulder straps. I was nervous. At age 28 this was my first backpack trip. My family car-camped when I was young, but I was never especially athletic. As we started up the trail, I realized that if we forgot something or I changed my mind, every outward-bound mile would have to be retraced. This was scary business. Only in the company of seven Carrie Nation Rises sisters would I venture onto that trail into the wilderness of the Trinity Alps. Two were experienced backpackers Although I was afraid I couldn't cut it on the trail, I was excited about spending three days together with these strong women in the quiet and beauty of the mountains.

It was the early 1970s, the feminist movement was in full swing, and consciousness raising was heady business. The five women of the ranch, Sue, Judy, Kathie, Bobi and I formed the Carrie Nation Rises with other friends. We wanted to bring movement issues to our politically conservative neighborhood and to fill our own needs for connection and relevance. Roughly fifteen women met every month in our living rooms, cross-legged on the floor, many smoking and drinking jug wine as we explored what it meant to be a woman in the 1970s. Careers, even working for a paycheck, were big issues for many in those days. I had just left a life as a stay-at-home wife and mother and gone to work for the local poverty program. My motives were to feed myself and my young son and to reduce my dependence on my ex-husband. If this were to be my new life, surely I needed longer term goals than identifying a new mate. Just exactly what those goals would be, and how I would figure them out: these were the dilemmas facing many women across the country who had been raised in the '40s and '50s. We were, in the midst of all this, immeasurably aided by the participation of Molly. She was twenty years older than the rest of us. She had struggled to make a life in a man's world as an architect. Success in her case was helped by a partnership with her husband, also an architect. Molly taught us that finding and keeping work was a task that could last a lifetime.

Kitty was a flamboyant blonde, with a raucous laugh and a forthright enjoyment of sex in all its forms. She was in a similar position to my own, having left her home, her husband – a prominent attorney – and her two young children, to move into a studio and determine whether her art could sustain her. This move was tragically cut short when her husband was diagnosed with brain cancer. She then moved to the task of supporting Bob and helping her children cope. Gail, who was discovering her calling as a reporter, was desperate to escape a failing marriage to an alcoholic and to find the courage to live independently with two small children.

We were stretching our bodies as we climbed the trail. It was not the first time we dealt with bodies together, of course. Bodies as viewed by others were a continuing topic. The Barbie doll defined a desirable body shape at the time, and miniskirts were just passing out of fashion. For some of us, the changes in our bodies caused by child-bearing were dispiriting. For others, those changes were a mark of pride. For Molly, our oldest member, they were viewed as inevitable, along with the sagging and wrinkling of age. We were even able to talk a little about masturbation, although I betray my age and upbringing by still feeling squeamish to even say the word.

Gail and I, the two with the most statuesque bodies, talked while we hiked about whether signing up as a feminist meant we had to lose our bras. We agreed that the sight of either of us bra-less would be like watching a litter of puppies under a blanket. Hair was a big issue for me as well. I have curly hair that frizzes in the slightest damp. I spent my teen years sleeping on orange juice cans as curlers. I hoped against hope that I would find a treatment that would deliver to me the hair of Grace Kelly or Jackie Kennedy. In those heady days of both feminism and anti-poverty organizing, someone told me I had cheek-bones like Kathleen Cleaver. She was a beautiful black woman and the wife of Black Panther Eldridge Cleaver. I immediately adopted an afro-like natural do, and have not changed it in forty years.

We had talked about bodies more intimately as well. Most of us had a newsprint copy of "Our Bodies, Ourselves." Even though many of us were married, several had children, and none of us thought we were innocent, we did think we ought to undertake that anatomical self-exam the book suggested. Giggling, sure it was foolish, we squatted over hand mirrors and took a look. We were surprisingly hairy and pouchy, as I'm sure our lovers and our gynecologists already knew. Gail tried hard to think of Georgia O'Keefe's lilies as we looked at our own vaginas. We did not use a speculum to probe even deeper, and we weren't ready to examine each other. But we did learn some things. The body exploration allowed us to talk more freely. Vibrators, for instance, were a tantalizing and risqué topic. Surprisingly, some described how they worked!

Why did we name ourselves for Carrie Nation, that axe-wielding, 19th century feminist and prohibitionist? Not in honor of prohibition, for sure. A curiosity in a small town, we were invited to explain ourselves to an all-male bastion, the Redding Rotary Club. Elected to speak for the local Women's Movement group, I was consciously provocative, using the f-word at least once. At one memorable moment a short, round man challenged me: weren't there a lot of jobs that women weren't meant to hold? "I don't know," I answered, "but do you want to arm wrestle?" He retired to his seat with a red face, recognizing that I had 20 years and several inches on him. The story, of course, made the rounds of this small town. A male columnist from the local daily paper, an ex-logger, wrote a glib, insulting piece wondering where we would choose to burn our bras. We phoned the paper and announced to the editor that we were on our way to the editorial room in our mini-skirts and packing our chain saws. We were coming to saw the offending columnist's desk in half. Thus the name of our group, the Carrie Nation Rises, was born. The paper thereafter assigned all coverage of the women's movement to Gail, reporter and charter member of the Carrie Nation.

We read the feminist texts together for our meetings: Simone de Beauvoir, Betty Friedan, Germaine Greer, Mary Wollstonecraft, Erica Jong. We explored fully the issue of sex (Kitty saw to that!). Those of us who were coupled with men promised them earnestly, and with our fingers crossed behind our backs, that we never, ever talked about their specific penis. In those pre-AIDS, post-1960s days, most of us, married or no, had explored sexually, some with spousal consent, some without. Of course, so had our partners, all too often. We talked and talked about the realization that an affair neither fixed a marriage nor necessarily replaced it. On the other hand, learning about an affair after the fact still felt like betrayal. Agreeing to freedom before the fact did not lessen the emotional impact either. I recognized that my own affair with a political figure while working on campaigns out of town was thrilling, but not a relationship to build a life around. Why was I so wounded by my then-husband's infidelity with a woman I knew? Molly provided the challenging discovery that storms and jealousies would not magically end on our 30th birthdays. She also taught us how to love and accept the males in our lives while we struggled to be ourselves. She counseled, "Let there be space in our togetherness." So many of us were wounded by our experience with affairs of the heart; she offered the wisdom and strength to forge new relationships. Lines in the face and sags in the body parts were in our future. She demanded that we face our lives with honesty and forgiveness, for ourselves and each other.

I really did not think I could manage the climb that first day of the hike. For a sedentary, storytelling smoker the hike was sweaty and the pack was so heavy it chafed my shoulders. My feet hurt in my new boots, but I didn't have the breath even to complain. Early in the trip, I faced terror. Slightly acrophobic, I felt my knees turn to jelly as the trail wound around the lip of a cliff high above a roiling, foaming waterfall. But these were my sisters, and if they could do it, I at least could try. Holding the hand of a similarly weak-kneed sister, we planted our butts against the rock wall behind us and edged our way to safety. Conquering this fear gave me courage and strength to go on. At one break, I dropped my pack and stepped off the trail to pee. I found a pile of rocks to balance against in this seemingly pristine mountain wilderness. I soon realized with astonishment that I had come upon the foundation of an old cabin, likely from the Gold Rush days in the 1860s or 1870s. This land had seen not just Indians and, possibly, fur traders, but miners and in some cases their families. Did some 19th century woman try to turn this wild country into home a hundred years before? The thought made the land less threatening and the sisterhood more precious.

Mid-afternoon, we reached a place along the creek where boulders formed a wide pool of turquoise water. Kitty and Sue, our most experienced hikers, announced that we should camp here. I dropped that pack with glee. Along with the others, I shed all my clothes for a skinny-dip in a blissful, cool, refreshing bit of paradise. We had done it, we had done it together, and we were sharing the rewards of that effort. Splashing in the snow-fed water, we heard the crunch of footsteps along the trail. Everyone suddenly stopped giggling and dodged behind the huge leaves gracing our pool. Everyone, that is, but Gail, who had just shed her swimsuit and reserve for the first time. She was on all fours, intent on a climb up a rocky bank. There, between her hands, was a pair of battered, lace-up boots, topped by government-issue pressed green pants. They were on the feet of a trail ranger. "May I see your wilderness permit, ladies?" Gail told the young ranger, who was grinning broadly, "I don't have it on me." She asked him to take it out of her pack. "I couldn't possibly go through your private things," he said. Gail looked him over for a long minute. Then, while her sisters cowered behind their leaves, she stood up, buck naked, and walked slowly to her pack to extract the permit. Proud and challenging, comfortable in the sisterhood we had found in those living room talks, in those public presentations, and in the shared experience of mountains, she was something. We were something.

That evening taught me more of the joys of backpacking. We satisfied our hard-earned hunger with trout that Gail pulled from the creek. We laughed, relived the trail and the ranger visit and enjoyed brandy-laced mint tea made from Pennyroyal leaves picked along the trail. I was exhilarated to realize that I could spend time opulently with only as much stuff as I could carry. I was proud that the trail had been conquered, not fast and not as far as some, but far enough. We talked about our jobs a little bit; we talked some about politics. There was, after all, an unpopular war on overseas and a war on poor women here at home. We talked about our loves and challenges; we probably even talked about penises, at least in the abstract. Sleeping in the dirt or not, the night sky never looked more elegant or the sleep more beckoning than after that first day on the trail.

The next morning taught us all, again, the strength of sisterhood. Kitty's dog Samson came back from his dawn run exploring the neighborhood with a rapidly swelling lip, near his nose. Two red beads of blood shone a fang-width apart. Bobi investigated and found it was a fat timber rattlesnake. We did not know how a dog would deal with rattlesnake venom. However, the bite was close to his heart. We had to act. Samson was a beloved companion, not just for Kitty but for her two children, who were coping with a very sick father. This threat underscored all our vulnerabilities. We were scared. Maybe we weren't as powerful as we thought we were. Maybe we couldn't really conquer the wilderness, within ourselves or outdoors. Nonetheless, the group responded without hesitation. We detached Gail's pack from its old Kelty frame and strapped on Samson with a leather belt. Carrying the 80 pound Labrador on our makeshift litter and cooling his nose with bandanas dipped in the trailside creek, we double-timed it back down the mountain trail, trading off when we tired. The veterinarian in nearby Weaverville was waiting with an anti-venom shot after the call from the trailhead. Samson was treated and survived. When Kitty returned to the trailhead where we camped that night with the good news, we cheered and filled our tin cups several times as tension eased from our sore bodies. We could indeed face challenges and prevail. We could indeed rely on each other in the face of difficulty. Samson went on to join us on more backpacking trips, carrying his red pack that contained dog food on the way in and trash on the way out.

The sisterhood of the Carrie Nation made an indelible imprint on the structure of Big Wheels Ranch. Strong women demanded an equal say, and intolerance of male privilege was built into our relationships. In the earliest days, the youth of most of us likely made our feminism a little more shrill that we would be comfortable with today. But in fact, the sisterhood that we learned together has served us well in our lives together at the ranch.

OWNERSHIP

The call came to the ranch late in the evening. Sue's husband Chuck had either tried to drive his car head-on into a logging truck, or lost control of the car while drunk. It was never clear what caused the accident. However, he was badly hurt, maybe fatally. Ranch members drove Sue to the hospital, an hour away. Sue put all the anger and humiliation of the recent past into a box someplace and headed for Chuck's bedside. He was in a coma for more than a week and in the local hospital for more than a month. The logging truck had basically landed in his lap. He was to undergo several operations, and would be bed-ridden and then wheel-chair-bound for months afterward. He was treated for a complicated infection in the early days in the Redding hospital. When the local internist found that Chuck's blood work was unusual, he was sent to the Veterans Administration in the Bay Area, where a cancer was found that further complicated Chuck's limited recovery.

Chuck and Sue's marriage was in trouble. Chuck drank way too much and way too often. When he drank he became loud and verbally abusive. Living at the ranch at this time meant living much of the time within sight and hearing of other ranch members. More to the point, any antisocial behavior became an issue for more than the immediate family. By now, a couple of years into ownership of the ranch, three of the original purchasers had left and others had moved in. On this night, other ranch members objected to Chuck's loud and confrontational behavior at dinner. He slammed the door as he stormed out of the main house, climbed into his car and headed to the valley to see his mistress.

Underlying the immediate problem with drinking were other issues with Chuck. He was fifteen years older than the other adults at the ranch, raised in a different era, and expected different kinds of relationships, especially between men and women. He was a bully and believed that his words had special weight, especially with Sue and his children, Chris and Laurie. These teenagers also lived at the ranch. One of the initial members of the ranch, Kathie, had left altogether because of Chuck. She felt bullied and disempowered by him. She believed that he simply could not see any other vision or model for the ranch than his own. He did not respect the work that she and others did in town because it was not paid as well as his own. Kathie also believed that the other members of the ranch were too tolerant of Chuck's very male energy. Too many occasions at the ranch ended in tangled and unhappy interactions and Chuck was most often a part of the struggle.

Chuck was also a talented teacher and organizer. He was handsome, silver-haired and bearded, stocky. I especially learned a great deal from Chuck in my new employment at the poverty program. His friends from United Farm Worker organizing days, and from poverty program training seminars, were frequent visitors to the ranch and became inspirational guides to the political challenges we faced in the early 1970s. These friends and admirers rallied around after the accident and, along with ranch members, provided a way to deal with this devastating event.

The women at the ranch put out the call to the women's group, the Carrie Nation Rises. Chuck's ex-wife was notified (another angst-fraught exchange with a woman still angry that Chuck had married the much younger Sue). Chuck's mistress came up from Woodland to visit. Chuck's children were comforted. Friends in Redding provided a room for Sue, ensuring that she did not need to make the hour drive each way from the ranch to the hospital.

We all had some familiarity with coma. As part of the organizing with the local Indian occupation effort, we had come to know Richard Oakes. Richard was a leader in the Indian occupation of Alcatraz Island, and he had been an inspiration to the local Pit River tribe in their occupation of PG&E and US Forest Service land. Richard had been badly injured in a fight, hit in the head with a pool cue. He was in a coma for a month. Many of our local Indian friends had traveled to see him and believed that his recovery was related to constant conversation at his bedside. He's still there, they said about Chuck, and he will know that you are there even when he cannot acknowledge your presence.

So we organized the support teams. There was a lot of conversation and hugs for Sue and Chris and Laurie. There was a schedule of hospital visitors. I went for a piece of time every day, despite a longstanding fear of hospitals. Every day I would sit by Chuck's bed in the Intensive Care Unit and read out loud from the newspaper. I would report on the gossip from the poverty program office. Chuck did not respond to me or look at me directly. Ultimately, he began to babble in ways that did not respond to my conversation. However, confirming the advice we had gotten, the first time Chuck saw me after he came awake he thanked me for coming to visit him so often, and then he looked confused. "You did, didn't you?" he asked.

More concrete help and resources came from all over the state. Architect friends from Redding designed a very small house next to the main house so that Chuck and Sue could move from upstairs to a more manageable place. Friends from Chuck's United Farm Worker organizing days brought a crew of builders to the ranch to raise the house in a matter of days. We built a covered ramp from the new house so that he could move to the main house for meals and socializing when he was in his wheel chair.

The ranch as a whole faced a more substantial challenge, however. Chuck was one of the main contributors to the monthly mortgage payment. The ownership structure at the time was a traditional land purchase agreement: the initial purchasers paid in a combination of down payment and monthly payments. Those who had left sold their shares to newcomers. Bill and I purchased a share when Pete left the Ranch. We still lived in town, but spent vacation and family time at Big Wheels Ranch. The "shares" in the enterprise that these payments provided were complicated, but carefully noted. The bottom line, however, was that Chuck's share of the monthly amount owed to the bank could not be comfortably replaced. It was possible that this one accident could result in losing the ranch.

We were, however, to be saved. One of the new non-owner residents of the ranch was Judy, an organizing colleague and friend of Sue's from college and Students for a Democratic Society (SDS) organizing days. Judy existed with a hole in her heart, literally, in the days before surgery could remedy such a problem. She had already lived past her expected life span. Sue has a vivid memory of her first understanding of the health issues Judy lived with. On a cross country trip with college friends, they stopped to swim in a river. Everyone else jumped into the clear and refreshing water; Judy did not. "Don't you swim?" Sue asked. "If I jumped into cold water, my heart would likely stop." Judy loved the land of the ranch and worked tirelessly in the garden and orchard. All of my memories of Judy include her hands, dirty from work in the garden. Slow, but very determined and very fierce, are the adjectives that describe her work, whether organizing or gardening. She took careful samples of every tree in the orchard and took them to the crop experts at the University of California, Davis, for identification. She was profanely scornful of those who planted the red delicious trees, and other "easy, trash apples." For that matter, she was profanely scornful when I told her I admired her as a farmer. "Why would you identify anyone by their occupation," she wondered, "instead of more human and basic qualities?" I was abashed. The exchange prompted me to question my own focus on work as the defining ingredient of adult life. One ranch resident described her as "the real deal:" a woman who lived her principles.

Judy's parents stepped into the crisis caused by Chuck's accident. A labor lawyer and Democratic activist who lived in Colorado, they were close to and supportive of Judy in all her adventures, but not overbearing. They had taken Judy to the Mayo clinic as a young child and done what they could to be sure she was as healthy as possible. Beyond that, they believed that the ranch was a good and stable place for Judy and wanted it to stay that way. They paid off the mortgage at the bank, requesting that payments continue to be paid to them. It worked, and there was comfort in knowing that foreclosure was not going to happen.

The ranch survived Chuck's accident. More than seven months later, Chuck and Sue returned from the veteran's hospital in the Bay Area, moving into the new little red house adjacent to the main house. Sue had spent those seven months not thinking about the future, simply focusing on the day at hand. When they returned to the ranch, she believed she could re-engage in her marriage and devote herself to Chuck's recovery. In some ways, the ranch provided the space for Chuck to heal. Good friends, welcoming spaces, and the knowledge that his lifetime of organizing had provided pals with the skills and commitment to build a place for him no doubt helped.

Despite this, Chuck and Sue's marriage ended. It may be that group living made the strains in the marriage obvious. It may be that the solidarity of the women's group allowed Sue to act to meet her own needs. Sue acknowledged her own lesbian inclination and began a relationship in the Bay Area. She moved to Redding for a bit, then on to the Bay Area to pursue her own academic career. She remained a member of the ranch, spent vacations there, and returned to live there full time in her retirement. Chuck found that even with the willing help of ranch members, he could not manage comfortably at the ranch. Although he could move around some on his own, he spent most of his time in a wheel chair. He moved to Fresno to live with organizing colleagues and to attempt to put a relationship together with his mistress. When that failed, he met, and ultimately married a new love and lived the rest of his life in the Bay Area with her.

Judy's final gift to the ranch was a big one. She died of a heart attack in her bed at the ranch. We'd all like to think that it was easy, but how is one to know? She had recently been for one of her regular visits to the University of California-San Francisco medical center. They put her on a new medication that she knew signaled the end. She tried to talk to friends about this; not everyone was ready to face the truth. More than her gardening skills, to this day we miss her acerbic tongue and her willingness to look at every issue directly, speaking truth not just to power but to her friends. She reoriented my view of work as a defining personal identifier; her directness had that effect on others as well. Judy's parents sent a note to the ranch expressing their gratitude for a good life here, and announced that they had burned the mortgage. They suggested, but certainly did not demand, that Fred, a close friend to Judy and a man with very few resources, be admitted as an owner.

So the ranch was now owned free and clear by a specified group of people, some who lived on the ranch and others who had moved on but still had shares, still others like Bill and I who had purchased the share of an original owner. The ownership was a complex structure that figured individual shares based on financial contributions. There were a variety of ownership challenges in addition to the oddness of owning something like 6/49 of a piece of land. We had been lucky in the marital breakups, including Chuck and Sue's. Whatever the personal pain and animosity, none of the departing folks used a monetary share of the ranch as a bargaining chip. Indeed, those that left had so far been patient about receiving their share over a long and sometimes raggedy repayment period. Could we count on this? What if a departing resident was personally financially desperate? What about our minor children? If I were to drive into a logging truck, would my ex-husband ignore this asset for our son Ben's future? How would we value those shares anyway? If we used current land values, the shares of early owners would be significant and would only grow. It was time, and probably past time, to reconsider our ownership structure.

We discussed the structure for months and months. Indeed, some aspects of the discussion go on today. We finally created an Unincorporated Association called Big Wheels Ranch. We divested ourselves of ownership in the land, and recorded title in the name of the Association. One simple benefit of this arrangement was to untangle the complicated list of owners, past owners, divorced owners, grown children, non-owner residents and any others who might claim a share from the land title. Generally, we make decisions by a three-quarters majority of those present at a formal ranch meeting. However, adding new members, adding any permanent new building, permanently expelling any member, or selling all or part of the property all require unanimous approval. Couples are identified as members individually. We have said in the by-laws that membership is not inheritable. This provision has not been tested. We also fixed specific dollar amounts for original shares in the Association, in amounts equal to the dollars contributed. These shares, with no increase due to changes in the value of the property or inflation, can be requested in the event a member leaves. If the ranch is sold, an unlikely event, the original shares will be repaid first, in the dollar amounts listed, with the balance then shared equally among all members. Members who have joined since the Association became our structure have donated money and work in various amounts. But their donations have not been added to the indebtedness of the original shares.

It is unusual in the 21st century to have a large and valuable resource with little or no current value to owners. Membership in the ranch cannot be considered an investment in the usual sense. In fact, there is no individual ownership of specific houses. Ranch members are, however, respectful of the building or improving or simply long-term occupation of the houses on the ranch. The main house, the original 1920s-era farmhouse that was the only residence when we first bought the ranch, is now a gathering place, kitchen for group meals, and guest place, with no permanent resident. The most important discovery for those of us who live here, however, is the emotional support this community provides. It is a more than adequate substitute for an individual deed. If I start to feel anxious about the non-traditional structure of the ranch, I remember the family support provided Chuck, Sue, Chuck's children, and Judy and believe that community might just carry us through.

LIVING TOGETHER

In late winter 1985, I walked slowly downstairs in the main house for the regular quarterly meeting of the Big Wheels Ranch Association. Although I was a member, I did not live at the ranch and my back hurt from the nearly four hour drive from Sacramento. Now, as a grey rain drizzled outside, the thought of the tense and angry discussion to come made my stomach hurt as well.

At issue was whether to accept Kansas, and his wife Robin and son Cimarron, as permanent residents of the ranch. At that point, they had lived at the ranch for two-and-a-half years and the question of whether or not to grant them permanent status had dominated our meetings for at least a year.

Kansas was a gifted mechanic who kept his own and others' machinery running. But he was also a prima donna who refused to do his share of the less glamorous cooking and cleaning that the rest of us felt must be equally shared. Early on, Sue had captured our fundamental philosophy precisely when she said there was no Daddy chair at the Big Wheels table. Kansas didn't get it, and it made the rest of us angry.

We gathered in a circle of ratty chairs in the living room of the main house. Kansas sat a little back from the main circle. He was a strong-featured man, with the ropy body of a man who works with his hands. He was bright and articulate. Robin was more comfortable, probably because her behavior was not the center of the discussion. She was a vibrant woman, with dark hair, a quick smile, and a loud laugh. She was mostly quiet in this meeting, a rare choice for her. Cimarron, a preschooler, played upstairs with the rest of the children. It was chilly and a fire had been built in the wood stove. We were still only part way through the job of replacing windows and doors in the early 20th century main farm house, and it was always chilly when the wind blew. Over the course of the day, breaks had to be taken regularly to make up for the uncomfortable chairs and the lack of activity. Coffee, food, and trips to the single bathroom broke up the meeting. Children needed to be comforted, tended to, and fed. Still, we met for roughly five hours: no one could enjoy this. It is a heavy price to pay for living as a group.

We began the meeting as we always did, with brief comments by everyone present. Usually, this was a time to catch up on family news, health issues, even reports on the neighboring community. It was a measure of the tension in the air that no one had the stomach for this family-building exercise. So we began with a request that each person give, without interruption, a point of view on the issue of Kansas and his family remaining at the ranch.

Those who had been at the ranch for extended periods while Kansas and family lived there, especially the women, complained that Kansas did not take his turn at either cooking or cleaning the main house. The general issue of whether some kinds of work (machinery or wood cutting, for instance) were more important to the group than other work (cooking and cleaning) was fundamental for many who lived at the ranch. We tried to operate so that no one could claim a special authority (especially not a male authority) because of the kind of work they did. There was no question that Kansas' mechanical skills were important. There was also no question that the ranch was based in part on the notion that everyone has to participate in the less glamorous parts of living. Kansas argued that his time was better spent doing something else. He offered to hire someone to clean the kitchen for him (no doubt a girl). Over the previous year, he had repeatedly promised to do his share. At the next meeting, Kansas would have done whatever he wanted and that did not include his share of the scut work. The meeting got even more tense, if that was possible.

Fred, whose skill level with tools matched that of Kansas and who had a strong commitment to maintaining the physical infrastructure of the ranch, complained that Kansas did not return the communal tools to the tool shed. Despite this, Kansas' car repair tools were off limits to others. No matter the need for more skills and more hands to maintain the ranch, Fred said that Kansas did not play well with others.

Barbara, resident and lawyer who had done much of the work on our articles of association and by-laws, reminded everyone that the law relating to tenants and landlords applied to the ranch. Continued residence by anyone for long periods of time granted the resident a right to continue, even if membership was not formally granted. Kansas and Robin and Cimarron had lived at Big Wheels for more than two years. At some point, and we had probably reached that point, Kansas and his family could require that we undertake a formal eviction action. Such an action could jeopardize the legal structure of our Association. It certainly would threaten our self-image as a community. It was past time to either formalize their status or ask them to leave. They could be identified as 'permanent residents': this would require the consent of those already living at the ranch. Or, they could be admitted as full members of the association, which would provide them with a right to the assets of the ranch in the event it was ever dissolved, and would provide a right to visit or live at the ranch any time. This membership status would require unanimous consent of the existing members, those resident and not.

Peter, Barbara's husband and also a lawyer, was protective of Kansas. Although he did not claim special status on his own behalf, he often felt that the militant feminism of some members of the ranch made it hard for men to live here. He felt that the group as a whole was bullying Kansas. Peter was joined by Chris, who had been suspended from the ranch for a two-year period. Although that period was over and Chris was again a full member, he felt that his own status as a ranch member remained tenuous. Asking anyone to leave the ranch was difficult for Chris.

Marty, a young resident, had very specific issues that made Kansas' status at the ranch complicated. He and his partner had led the effort to purchase a redwood water tank from the Bay Area. They developed the plans to turn the structure into a two story shop and home, and had received approval from the membership to put the new structure at the end of the orchard near the main house. Kansas dreamed of operating an auto repair business on the first floor. More to the point, he and Robin loaned the ranch money to build the foundation and cement slab floor, finish the roof and provide for interior finishing. Kansas especially, but Robin as well, had worked many hours with other ranch members to build this new addition. On the other hand, Marty, more than any other ranch member, hated conflict and hated meetings. He agonized at this meeting, appreciating Kansas' skills and work on the tank house, but also hating the continual conflict that Kansas' residency caused for residents and members alike. Ultimately, Marty and his partner would leave the ranch, unwilling to participate in the negotiation and struggle that group living required.

Sue, original ranch member and the treasurer at the time, raised the unhappy issue of money. Ranch finances were challenging. In fact, ranch finances have been challenging for most of our time together. Life in rural America has been cash – and job – poor for a long time. But in the early 1980's when this meeting occurred, times were especially hard at Big Wheels. The ranch membership was still paying off the contributions from two members who had left the association. Difficult financial times in the larger economy meant that many members, resident and non-resident alike, were slow in paying quarterly tax, insurance, and special project fund payments. It was not clear that we had the capacity to repay the loan for the tank house from Kansas and Robin. Sue's defense of the principles that all work was valuable and that assignments of work needed to be negotiated in a group was fierce; her feminism was without question and the struggle over whether we would have a Daddy with special authority had originated with her ex-husband Chuck. However, she cautioned that there would be consequences if Kansas and Robin left.

The pieces of the puzzle were obvious. Only a couple of years before this meeting, the number of people living on the ranch was down to three. All the members were worried that we would be

unable to maintain the property. We had over the last year needed
to repair a collapsed bridge across the creek and repair the roof in
the main house. We faced the requirement to upgrade the bathroom
in the main house, maintain the irrigation system, garden, and
pasture. The three who remained on the ranch in the recent past
were not exactly angry, but at least grumpy, at the expectation that
they would pick up the slack to protect the investment of absentee
owners. When Kansas and his family arrived, both the additional
person-power and money, however modest, were sorely needed.

Like Marty, I have always been averse to conflict. The room was
too warm by the middle of the afternoon and we all were beginning
to smell of the sweat that tension brings. Too much coffee made my
morning stomach ache worse. I was especially fond of both Robin
and Cimarron, and had a hard time imagining an eviction. It seemed
like we were just recovered from the group damage done when we
asked Chris to leave some years before. More recently, we were
recovering from a period when the residents on the ranch were too
few to maintain themselves and the land easily. What were a few
dirty dishes and un-mopped floors worth, anyway?

But neither side in this debate could give in. Kansas could
not commit to community decision-making over how he spent
his time, especially if his skills were considered equal to those
of a housekeeper. Others, myself included, could not give up on
a commitment to equal value for all kinds of work. At the end of
the meeting we had reached agreement only on a timetable. By
September, we would come to a final decision on the status of Kansas
and his family. They would be asked to leave, accepted as permanent
residents or, become full Association members.

By September, Kansas, Robin and Cimarron left the ranch.
Eviction was not required; neither was a formal vote at a quarterly
meeting. Robin and Cimarron have maintained a relationship with
the ranch over the years, visiting and, in Cimarron's case, building

lasting relationships with the other young people who grew up at the ranch. Kansas and Robin divorced not long after they left the ranch. But the functioning of the ranch as a voluntary family was strained by the experience. Lynn, spending the school year in the Bay Area working toward her therapist's license, arranged for a mediator to help us all find our way back to workable family relationships. As for me, I learned that some kinds of tension can be as destructive as a single big fight. Long, tense meetings that grind away at the participants are indeed a high price to pay for living together. We have to resolve the problems that are inevitable in any relationship. However, we will not stay together if we cannot find a way to assure that our time together has some rewards as well as trials. For some of the people who have lived here, the requirement to meet and to submit decisions to a group process was not worth it. For me, the meetings are worth the trouble, and I will choose to endure, even to initiate, a specific conflict rather than a slow and repeated grinding away at our relationship.

Holidays in the 'Hood

I stepped into Jimmy's arms for a waltz in the crowded living room at Piltdown Ranch. The wood stove kept the indoors toasty. It was New Year's Eve in the late 1970's and, as in most years, we were gathering at Ed and Ray's for a raucous celebration of the past year and a hopeful toast to the year to come. We all had had our share of Ray's signature drink: a White Russian made with cream milked from the cow that morning. Dinner, as always at Ed and Ray's, was very late. It was a race to see if we would have it on the table before the New Year actually arrived.

Jimmy was black, gay, overweight, middle-aged. He was an unlikely visitor to this rural mountain community. He was a museum professional, a wicked gossip, and an old friend of Ed and Ray's from the bright lights and big city of the Bay Area. He was a trained classical singer and a real dancer who strained my own abilities.

What a feast we were to have! Ray was cooking a roast on the wood kitchen stove, and I was studiously avoiding asking which of the cows had given its all. I knew those cows from the week my husband and I had provided ranch-sitting duties while Ed and Ray travelled to the desert for a brief vacation. On this occasion, Jimmy and I had collaborated on Hoppin' John and greens, the pairing that both my husband Bill, a transplanted white South Carolinian, and Jimmy, a black Marylander, believed would guarantee prosperity in the new year. Jimmy added corn bread from his mama's recipe and quince jam from local trees. Lynn, the premier baker in the neighborhood, had provided a spectacular carrot cake. And all the other 30 or more neighbors and friends had brought contributions of food and drink to share.

As midnight approached, we put on boots and jackets over our finery and made our way through the gently falling snow to the hill behind the house. No lights are visible from Ed and Ray's hill, except their own cabin. We could hear the gurgle of the ditch that feeds the water system from a spring to the house. Ed, who was raised on this 160 acres settled by his parents in the 1940s, had built an enormous bonfire. Ed fired off the old ranch rifle at midnight, the gun looking as though it might have arrived on a covered wagon. We sang and passed around champagne bottles for direct swigs, until cold hands and feet drove us indoors. It being the 1970s and all, our songs leaned heavily toward civil rights and anti-war songs, a lot of Woody Guthrie and Pete Seeger. As the evening got later, we drifted into the old camp songs we had learned in our childhood.

Thirty-some years later, this annual holiday ritual is a warm and favorite memory. It is also a vibrant continuing tradition. Holiday celebrations represent much of the reason we have, I believe, lasted as a community. And some of these memories are, of course, bittersweet. Ed and Ray are gay men who have thrived in this conservative and rural community. In part this is because of the respect that local folks have for anyone who can survive ranching cattle on small acreage; in part because Ed, whatever his personal life, is a local boy; in part because together they may be the best hosts in the area. But AIDS took a fearful toll among their larger circle of friends and acquaintances in the years after the late 1970s. Divorce and remarriage took many of that New Year's participants elsewhere, and brought in new folks to the circle. To some extent, we all paid the piper for the explosion of sexual exploration in the 1960s and 1970s. It turned out that freedom and even license brought risks and heartbreak for many of us.

It turned out, as well, that we were not immune after all to demographics. My dance partner Jimmy died in 2014 of some version of congestive heart failure. He had moved to our neighborhood in retirement. He lived comfortably in this conservative area. The libertarian ethic here apparently allowed someone of his color and sexual preference to find a place. He avoided the AIDS of so many of his friends in the Bay Area, but he did not avoid the toll taken by his genetics and sedentary lifestyle. Ed and Ray have given up hosting the annual New Year party, as they have changed the eating and drinking habits that threatened them as well. My knees require waltzing at a much slower pace these days. However, our grown children have taken charge lately. They build the bonfire, pass round the bottles of champagne, and even know the words to most of the Pete Seeger songs, as we gather down the road at David and Jaci's house now. We may think of those no longer around the circle, but we rejoice in community and still ring in a hopeful New Year.

FRED

Fred swirled onto the dance floor at the dome, ankle-length skirt moving to the rhythms of Creedence Clearwater Revival. It was Saturday night at the ranch. We were celebrating the end of the work week and the arrival of Fred's new sound system. After a long and careful building period, Fred's geodesic dome was beginning to feel like home. Fred was not a handsome man. He was tall and very thin with angular features and skin that never seemed to tan but burned regularly. For all his height, he faded into the background in most public settings and he rarely chattered. On this night, his jerky dancing made him resemble a scarecrow. Fred had just come out as a gay man. His joy in his new freedom, including the swirly skirt, was wonderful to watch, despite the poor dancing. The timing of his coming out, late in the 1970's, could not have been worse.

Fred arrived in our area when he left the Air Force in the mid-1970s. He first lived for a few weeks nearby in a community called Smith Camp, a squalid area of trailers and poor folks. The young people living at the ranch brought him to live at Big Wheels, a little like a puppy. He had not gone to Vietnam; he spent his war years unloading body bags at Vacaville. He was emotionally wounded when he arrived at our ranch, and not just by the enormous impact of dealing with the human cost of the war. In the Air Force he came face to face with corruption and human greed when he discovered coffins and body bag shipments used for smuggling drugs.

Fred's relationship with Judy helped this Ohio blue-collar boy find peace with who he was. Judy was, like Fred, fiercely committed to the ranch's particular 40 acres. Her directness and radical politics probably helped Fred sort out his own return to civilian life. I never knew if their relationship was physically intimate, but Fred shared, or adopted, or learned, Judy's politics as well as her commitment to a straightforward presentation of who she was.

Fred's sense of humor together with an unforgiving loyalty to tribe and family contributed to the ranch's reputation in the neighborhood. The ranch endured a long, contentious relationship with our northernmost neighbor. Al was an assistant county counsel in the Shasta County government and a fundamentalist Christian. When he left the county office, he represented many Christian groups as a private attorney in lawsuits about prayer and religious symbols in the public square. It was a difficult relationship for our group of lefties, some of them dope-smokers. Ranch members believed that Al called in the sheriff's team in the mid-1970's that busted one of the youngest residents for a small marijuana plot on Pacific Gas & Electric land nearby. Afterwards Fred put up an enormous sign in the meadow facing Al's horse barn: "Prosecutors Will Be Violated."

Fred was hostile to corporations, represented in our area by big timber companies and PG&E, builder of dams and transmission lines. Some of his hostility was driven by his experience of the appalling cost of the Vietnam war, in economic and human treasure. He had also adopted the fierce preservation ethic and anarchism of such people as Edward Abbey. For years, Fred manipulated our electric meter to reduce the readings from PG&E and hence the monthly bill. During Fred's tenure at the ranch, a low level of monkey-wrenching aimed at PG&E went on in the neighborhood: sugar in the gas tanks of equipment and stakes and property markers moved around on projects. There was no evidence that Fred was involved in these activities, but considerable evidence that he relished the damage every time it happened.

Fred was hard-working, central to establishing the infrastructure of the ranch as we know it. He rebuilt the 75-year-old irrigation system to reestablish a pasture that would support animals and a garden. He built a dam on the creek that would assure water high enough to maintain irrigation. The dam stands today, although its moveable boards to raise the creek level are not often inserted. My son Bayliss remembers Fred's determination to leave the ranch in tidy condition when Fred prepared to move to San Francisco. Fred rented a big dump truck, enlisted help from others including Bayliss, loaded up all the rubble abandoned by Marty when he left the ranch, and drove it to Marty's new house. Bayliss would have been offended at the implied criticism, but Marty appeared to be grateful to see all his treasures.

Fred's signature achievement was a geodesic dome to live in. He took a carpentry class at the local community college to upgrade his skills. He wrote for plans for the dome and painstakingly cut its individual wooden triangular panels. Built without plumbing or electricity, it was a handsome structure. It had pulleys to open upper vents for air circulation. It was also a frustrating building, since any problem with siding or windows required an individually fabricated repair, as each panel was different. It stood for thirty years. Finally it collapsed in a snowstorm that laid down 5 to 6 feet of very wet snow. No one had lived full time in the dome for many years, but for many owners and visitors it was a cozy hideaway in the tall trees. The dome was a pleasure despite using a composting 55-gallon barrel outdoors for a toilet and an extension cord from the nearest house for electricity. Today, the space where the dome sat is an impromptu garden where daffodils herald the spring each year, encircled by the concrete perimeter beam Fred laid down.

Most of Fred's 'gayness' happened out of our sight. Before he came out as gay, probably even to himself, he had a girlfriend down the road while living at the ranch. One of his local women friends describes him as like a girlfriend, with unusual gifts as a confidant. One of my fondest memories of Fred was a gift from him toward the end of his life. At a time when he had little money and less energy, he sent a book he found at City Lights Bookstore in San Francisco. It was a history of personal and political scandal in the City during the Gold Rush, and it reminded him of me, with my job in politics and taste for mysteries. He was a strong and loving friend, but struggled to form lasting romantic attachments. In retrospect, his reluctance to recognize his gayness was characteristic of most of our generation, raised in the '40s and '50s. I did not grow up understanding, or even imagining, a gay culture. Neither, I'm sure, did Fred. I credit him with teaching me that a gay preference means almost nothing about other parts of life. Fred chose a gay life at a certain point, although he did not choose his sexual makeup. He also chose to be an infrastructure expert at the ranch; he chose to be a loving and careful friend. He was unique, not a caricature. His model helped me stay calm and connected when my youngest son Bayliss came out some years later.

Fred was excited to come out as gay, and made many trips to the Bay Area where he found a social circle. Remembering Fred recalls the liberation and freedom of those early days. Drag queen performances were exuberant and playful. Halloween brought costumed extravaganzas in the Castro District. The bars and bathhouses provided opportunities to explore every variety of gay sexual expression. Women had experienced a decade of similar freedom in the 1960s. Then, pills and rock and roll made sexual experimentation possible without the life-altering risk of pregnancy. Most of us tried various new versions of adulthood: open relationships, clandestine affairs, or multiple partners. The celebration of gay experience in the 1970s seems like the same discovery.

It is also important to remember the very real threats that gay expression posed in the 1970s. At the end of the decade, Mayor George Moscone and Supervisor Harvey Milk of San Francisco were assassinated by Dan White. The reasons for White's shocking actions are tangled, but Milk's exuberant gay politics and Moscone's support for those politics were a part of his animus. Moscone was a friend and political colleague of mine. He had campaigned in our part of the world when he ran for governor in 1970. His loss was personal. For gay folks in Shasta County, local experimentation was just as risky, if not more so. Indeed, a well-known gay couple from the area were killed some years later by a pair of brothers who also bombed three Jewish synagogues and an abortion clinic in Sacramento.

Despite the danger, San Francisco held out acceptance, excitement, flash and dazzle. Fred came out, at the very time when no one knew the full consequences of unprotected sex and many, many partners.

Fred was diagnosed with HIV in the 1980s. It is as difficult to recapture the early days of the AIDS epidemic as it is to recapture the exuberant freedom of the 1970s. AIDS was mysterious, referred to in the press as the gay plague. It took years to determine how it was transmitted. It took even longer to develop treatments for the range of symptoms that the disease caused, from rare cancers to pneumonias. A cure eludes us today, although treatments allow people to live with HIV and a cure seems tantalizingly close. The Reagan administration in the 1980s in Washington did not help the situation. Reagan could not even say the word. The government did not focus research efforts on the disease for years. Some viewed AIDS as a heavenly judgment on an aberrant lifestyle. Large numbers of very sick young people overwhelmed the health system in San Francisco. People like Fred, with circles of friends in the Bay Area, watched with horror as many, many died. The wild party stopped abruptly. People avoided restaurants for fear of catching the disease. Sick individuals were fired from jobs and evicted from housing. Friends and family moved into the crisis to offer help and support. Lesbians in particular stepped forward to care for the sick and dying, overcoming years of suspicion and distance in the equality movement.

Fred approached his illness with the same care that he had used to build his dome. He moved to an apartment in the Bay Area to be closer to well informed medical care. He monitored his T-cell counts and tried the newest medications. He adjusted the medication as his blood tests dictated and he supplemented traditional medicine with alternative treatments. Life was, as always, financially difficult. He worked part time doing computing and he juggled credit cards to continue to afford his very expensive medication. He lived for a long time with the knowledge that his illness was terminal. He did not live long enough for medication and treatment regimes to catch up. For others, AIDS would later change from a death sentence into a chronic illness.

The ranch community, and many in his wider circle of friends, rallied around as he grew more frail. This circling of friends happened for many who suffered from AIDS. Health care settings opened up visiting hours, developed more hospice services, and recognized that people who were sick and dying needed community as much as medicine. Fred was not close to his birth family, although both his brother and mother came to visit toward the end of his life. A broad support group formed for him. We organized formally when people were available to sit and talk with him and identified who could provide financial help if necessary. The Fred support group developed a phone tree to share information so that Fred did not need to repeat and repeat his medical status. Friends he trusted came forward to provide the most intimate of personal support in his final weeks. He was skeletal at the end, and wanted help, at least emotional support, in his dying. No birth family member was present at the end. I was there, along with several other ranch members, to be sure he did not die alone. His pain and the confusion caused by the morphine he used to somewhat reduce that pain were heart-breaking. Despite the sorrow of this end, no one could possibly want his suffering to continue. He was ready to move on.

We scattered his ashes on Mt. Shasta on a trail he loved to hike. Friends embroidered a square for the AIDS quilt that became a national way of honoring AIDS victims. My son and I found that square when the quilt was displayed in Washington DC. It was the last time the entire quilt was able to be displayed, because of its enormous size. However, I find him much more present in the infrastructure of the ranch, where his years of effort created a working environment. We miss him today as we maintain the irrigation system, the septic tanks, the water and electrical systems. We miss him when we pay the full amount of the PG&E bill each month. We miss him when we listen to Creedence Clearwater.

MAIN HOUSE CHANGES

At 7 a.m. on September 11, 2001, I stood on the front steps of the main house at the ranch, tapping my foot and steaming. By 10 a.m., I was convinced that Mac, the house renovation guy we had hired, was a terminal flake and a mistake. The whole weary process of finding competent, willing and available help in a rural area would need to begin again. At 10, he drove his pickup slowly down the driveway. "I can see by your face that you haven't had the television on, " he said. Television, hah! No one had a television hooked up at the ranch. A radio was possible, but I was only camping in the main house. No one lived there, it was available for guests, and I was staying just during the renovation. Everyone at the ranch was excited about this dramatic makeover of our nearly-80-year-old log cabin. I had taken on the task of supervising the work.

Being upset about a late start on September 11 was a little embarrassing, once I got over it. The planes had crashed into the towers and the world had changed. Living in a news-free zone, it took some time to realize what had happened. Shortly after Mac arrived, I spent a long time on the phone with son Bayliss, going to school in Boston. He was very rattled by the nearness of the horrific attack, and the emotional toll of the attacks finally sunk in for me.

But the ranch is a constant, in the landscape and in our lives. Change of all sorts comes and goes. We have had fires nearby, floods of the seasonal creeklet, and boot-swallowing mud. The wind has blown down trees and beetles have brought too many trees down. Right now, there was work to be done on this much-loved house. We moved on and so did the rest of the world.

The biggest part of this project was to be a new kitchen, back porch and deck along the west side of the house. What we had was a small, dark kitchen with a door to the main dining/living room and a door to the back porch. The plumbing was elderly and subject to leaks. Next to the kitchen was a musty pantry. The whole kitchen had rough wood counters and walls and very elderly flooring. It was a depressing room, with aging appliances, little light, and less room to work.

By 2001, three additional houses had been added to the ranch, in addition to the original log house, since we began in the early 1970s. Each of these houses included a kitchen and a bath. It was surprising to remember the early years of the ranch. In those days, the full-time population often rose to a dozen. Every meal was cooked in the tiny kitchen in the main house and showers were often graced with company when someone had to use the single toilet. The numbers went even higher when guests and members living in town arrived. We all must have been very young indeed.

Despite the glaring problems with the log house kitchen, improvement had been delayed over the past twenty years. There were the kitchen and bath areas added to the other houses, making it easier to live at the ranch, especially with young children. The number of people living at the ranch was reduced in the 1980s and 90s, so there was less pressure to remodel the main house. Money, or the lack of it, was always a challenge. My personal commitment to change that kitchen came when I opened the doors under the sink and a frog hopped out. I am as interested in wildlife as the next city girl visiting the country, but that was just too much. Bill W was as committed as I was. He was the one who often had to slide on his back in the inadequate area under the house to fix a leak or thaw frozen pipes. The floor was too close to the ground, and the whole area under the house was dark and crawling with spiders. Bill W recommended that we hire someone to do the renovation who had no claustrophobia and could tolerate black widow spiders.

Beyond the aging of the log house, reasons to renovate were abundant. The main house was, and is, the hub of the ranch. We meet there. We eat together for birthdays, for holidays, for season changes, to celebrate achievements and, sometimes, just because it has been a little too long since we last ate together. Guests stay there, allowing us to keep other housing modest. The family Monopoly set is there and there is often a puzzle set up for all to work on. If the main house were to be unusable, it would be more difficult to think of the ranch as a community instead of a rural subdivision.

It had taken the usual year for ranch members to decide on a course of action. The main house is a small two-story log house that dates to the 1920's. We imagine that the trees to build the house came from the property. We don't have a way of confirming this, but the fact that the property was logged in that era supports our belief. We had over the years re-stained and re-chinked those logs, replaced windows, refinished floors, and redesigned the bathroom area to separate the toilet area from the tub, shower, and sink. This made the bathroom more comfortable for a group. But eighty years of wind and weather had taken their toll. Bill C and I were beginning to think about retirement at the ranch. It was time to see if the main house could be made more livable and stable enough for another eighty years.

We had to do some basics before we started on the kitchen. We put on a new metal roof that provided fire safety as well as eliminating the leaks that had become a recurring problem. We added roof insulation. The most dazzling addition was two skylights that added light and air to the long second story room that provides a bedroom and child play area. I was the first to stay in the main house after the new metal roof was put on. I discovered one downside. A large black walnut tree shades the house in front. The falling walnuts in early autumn can convince a sleeping brain that the house is under artillery fire. Added to the nightmares about 9/11, my fall in the main house was not especially restful, despite the satisfaction of the improvements to the heart of the ranch.

On that September day, Mac did an arduous under-house examination. Some of the piers had to be strengthened, although the house was surprisingly stable. The worst news was that the main log across the back of the house was rotting. A large tree stump would need to be removed and the enormous log replaced. The log was huge, a reminder that this house was built by a logging family who settled here when the forest was whole and the pine and fir trees ancient. Replacement, of course, required time and house jacks.

The kitchen was to be the revolutionary change. We wanted to combine the kitchen and pantry into a single room stretching the width of the house. I asked Mac whether we could cut through the log wall between the two rooms without destabilizing the house. "Let's be clear," he said. "We can do whatever you want, as long as you are willing to pay the price. If you've got the money, I've got the skills." We compromised, with a wide arch that left enough logs to support that newly airy bedroom upstairs. We put in long counters so that several cooks could work at once and lots of cupboards. We tripled the amount of window area, so the kitchen has plenty of light and views of the creek and pasture beyond. The kitchen is now communal space, comfortable but efficient, and a part of our woodsy landscape.

We opened up the wall between the kitchen and the living/ dining area so that activities in each area can be shared. We gossip and catch up while food is prepared. We often set a table for 15 – 20 on special occasions, and the new space allows meal preparation, eating, and clean-up to be shared. We rebuilt the back porch with a screened area where we now eat in summer. We added a long deck along the west side of the house, with a sliding door to the dining area of the main room. The deck is also a nice area for a meal except in the hottest or coldest seasons, and provides spectacular sunset viewing year-round.

The renovation made clear how the original house reflected the times. The family that built this house was different in some significant ways from our batch of communards today. That small kitchen was very likely a unisex domain, with a farm wife and any female children preparing all the meals. Our need for space so several of us at a time, men and women both, can prepare grand feasts would surprise that farm wife. The small dark pantry was also more necessary when the produce and fruit from the ranch itself were a significant part of the winter food supply. We gather in the main kitchen for applesauce making and canning occasionally; Theresa uses it for mammoth salsa making days when tomatoes are to be had. But none of us preserve the bulk of our winter food, and the days are few and far between when the grocery store 15 miles away cannot be reached.

The whole orientation of the original house was toward the road. The biggest windows, upstairs and down, originally faced south where the view was past the orchard and toward the road. The road must have been more obvious when the house was built in the 1920's, as this land had been logged. Winters were often longer, wetter, and snowier than they are today. The road was dirt and the mail in the winter was sometimes delivered by snowshoe. Cars were a rarity. I think about that ranch wife, spending long days canning apples and pears and vegetables. Visitors would be a high point. Views of the forest, the wilderness, would have little appeal.

As we renovated the house, we reflected more than a need for a more flexible and sociable room arrangement. We also gather here in part to appreciate wilder or, at least, more natural views and experiences. So our kitchen windows overlook the creek and its tangled vegetation. Blackberry vines, dogwood and other brush lean over the creek, along with watercress and mint for the picking. We can view the meadow and the woods beyond on the other side of the creek. Ducks and geese land on the pond in the meadow, especially during spring and fall migration. Turkeys occasionally strut through. Owls and bats appear at night. Deer and rabbits sometimes graze in the meadow. From time to time a bear will wander through, checking on the ripeness of the apples. We have a different sensibility indeed in this 21st century. There is perhaps a metaphor in the initiation of the main house repairs on September 11, unintended but chilling nonetheless. We have greater need of respite from the machinery of our modern age.

RAISING CHILDREN

Children at the ranch are a story with two, or maybe three, chapters. In the earliest days of the ranch, several young people in their teens and earliest twenties lived there, some with parents and some without. A few children spent most of their childhood there. Others grew up with the ranch as a presence in their lives, with a family relationship to ranch members and frequent visits, or even stays, through their growing years. For most of us in our later years, those children are the best of what we have done.

The phone call came in mid-morning in the early 1970s. It was only due to one member's job as a reporter that the early warning was received. Sheriff's deputies were headed for the Roseburg timberlands bordering the ranch. Several of the young people living at the ranch knew exactly what that meant. Chris and his cousin Paul, Fred, and Marty had a garden plot of marijuana growing there.

These young adults had struggled for months with older ranch members over the issue of marijuana. Many of us had enjoyed it from time to time. However, the price of a bust could mean losing the land altogether, on top of jail or other penalties for individuals. Some of the older residents worked in politically sensitive jobs like the poverty program. Others organized against timber cutting, in antiwar efforts, and in support of civil rights. This activism made the ranch vulnerable to legal action. It was necessary to be careful and discrete about any drugs. To the young people, making marijuana illegal was unjust and foolish. The economics of growing and sharing marijuana were also important in this very poor neighborhood. The activists prevailed: in several tense and lengthy meetings, ranch members made strict rules about not growing marijuana on the property.

Our neighbor to the north was a fundamentalist Christian who worked as a deputy county counsel. Al had complained about nudity on our ranch, and no doubt was suspicious that sex might be going on among the unmarried. Fred in particular believed that Al was spying on the nearby grow. When the call came, Fred immediately warned his partners to keep away: the sheriffs were coming! Paul, however, was younger and more foolish. He could not bear to imagine losing a season's crop. So he raced out to the plot to salvage what he could, straight into the arms of the law. What was he thinking? Youth and optimism were to exact a heavy price.

Paul was arrested. He took the heat for the grow, apparently convincing the police and the district attorney that he alone was responsible for the crop. In the end, he served some time in the county jail. The ranch's relationship with Al was soured for all time. Oddly, in later years, Al's libertarian tendencies overcame his distaste for marijuana. After he retired from the county, he acted as lawyer for Tiny, the neighbor on the road who was the best known local drug dealer.

Paul's arrest was a sad day for the ranch and heart-wrenching for Paul and his girlfriend. They left the ranch once his sentence was served. The bust also brought to a head some collective response to the challenges of living with young people. It probably was the tipping point in a long effort to deal with Chris's habit of breaking things.

Chris was a tall and husky teen when he moved to the ranch, one of the first residents. He moved in with his father, Chuck, and stepmother, Sue. He was good with dogs and small children. He willingly, though not always competently, chipped in to whatever work project was underway. In those days, projects were many and various. Every house was heated with wood, and firewood collecting, chopping to appropriate size, and stacking was needed every year. Ditches needed to be constantly maintained. Culverts needed to be built and maintained to keep the driveway manageable. The old log main house, dating to the 1920's, required (and requires to this day) continual reinvestment to be habitable. New insulation, plumbing repairs, replacement windows and window frames, new roof, and re-chinking the old logs were needed. Cows and chickens and turkeys and a garden all needed irrigation and regular tending.

Despite his strengths, Chris' transit through his teen years was difficult. He struggled in school, and left for a time for an alternative school in Oregon where he received his GED. He lived for a time at the ranch, then moved out for a bit at 18 to play with a band in the neighborhood. Chris always played music, rock and roll guitar, with his band and on the ranch. He participated fully in the alternative life-style aspects of the neighborhood. He tells good stories now of playing at the Forked Horn bar just down the road in Montgomery Creek. Patrons rolled joints in between changing a baby's diaper on the bar.

Chris had all the work habits of many barely-grown people. He broke several pieces of expensive equipment through a combination of clumsiness and plowing-while-high. He scared the older, more sober workers. A legendary story of Chris at this time was of driving while loaded down into town on his way to a music gig in Redding. He managed to miss completely the fact that the light was red and plowed his old and dilapidated Volvo into a Cadillac stopped at the light. The owner of the Cadillac stomped back to Chris, reached into the window and punched him in the nose. When the police arrived, Chris climbed out of the car, blood streaming, to talk to them. He believed he was maintaining well enough, so he leaned back against his car, only to find that the car was 12 feet behind him. He landed flat on his back.

Ranch members met time and again to discuss how to deal with the problems raised by Chris's behavior and that of the additional young people living there as well. All the residents, and the non-resident members, talked and talked and talked. We were a family, weren't we? We weren't going to throw people over the side, were we? We couldn't afford to lose the ranch and we couldn't afford to replace equipment very often either. Rules were made about behavior. Resident and member meetings were held more often. Some of the young people left, angry or disappointed or simply in search of other pastures. Some of the older people questioned whether any of us had the energy to keep meeting, talking, living in tension. In the end, Chris was suspended from membership in the ranch. Every effort was made to maintain a relationship with Chris, despite the suspension.

Chris today is an accomplished mental health therapist. He has been married to one woman for longer than many of the ranch members. He is a father and grandfather, and fully participating member, if non-resident, of the ranch community. We seem to have come through this together as family.

Talking with younger ranch members, whose growing up years took place here, reflects experiences both similar to those of Chris and his cousin Paul, and not. Zack, now in his early 20s, has lived at the ranch most of his life. For most of his childhood, only two families lived at the ranch and both had young children. Zack's experience with living with other members of the commune is more like living with close neighbors. He has appreciated knowing all of us, is not embarrassed by the 'commune' aura, and does not feel judged or hemmed in by the larger membership. On the other hand, life as a teen in this rural and somewhat isolated area had its challenges. He went to high school an hour away in town and missed the casual social life most teens expect. He appreciates the woods and the natural setting, but his own taste is for more organized sports like soccer and baseball. He believes now that he won't return to a rural life when he is finished with his education. The lack of drama in Zack's account of growing up here is, in part, his nature. It also may reflect the changes in the rest of us. He believes that drama at the ranch these days has to do with aging, not growing up. I probably agree.

My youngest son, Bayliss, visited the ranch regularly throughout his life, but never lived here full time. Bill C and I moved to live at the ranch only recently, in retirement. However, Bayliss remembers winter days snowshoeing and sledding on the ranch and nearby. Many summers included the highlight of tubing and swimming in the Pit River. Easter egg hunts and big group dinners for no good reason except fellowship are a part of the ranch. Work projects to gather firewood, clear ditches, stain the main house, and many other tasks help keep the ranch healthy. Holidays have often taken place here. We all remember bringing Bayliss's friend William to the ranch when the boys were about 8 years old. Thanksgiving day began with catching and killing the big turkey we would have for dinner. William was not only appalled in his little urban soul, but he refused to eat dinner with assassins. Bayliss was equally appalled at William's behavior: "What do you think? They make those Chicken McNuggets you like so much out of flour and water?"

It seems likely that Bayliss' transit to adulthood as a gay man was helped by his close association with the ranch. The community is loving and accepting. More importantly, he spent every New Year's Eve from young childhood to leaving home at the annual party at Ed and Ray's ranch, gay men who live down the road and whose strength and warmth offer a strong counter to stereotypes about gay life. The experience of the ranch community gathering to support Fred as he dealt with AIDS was a challenge, but a family-building one. Sue's lasting relationship with Sorca and their marriage provide another reminder that families come in many shapes. Bayliss is a member in his own right now, and we are hopeful that the adventures of his two sons, Owen and Ezra, will be a strong and cheerful part of their lives as well.

They are indeed the best part of us, all those children of the ranch. They have grown into loving adults. We expect there will be another generation with memories of this place, as our grandchildren come to dinner, attend celebrations, swim in the pond, gather eggs from the chickens, and learn from our wider ranch family that there will always be a safety net in hard times. Strong, smart, healthy children are the most important product of this ranch enterprise.

LOGGING

We gathered for our regular Association meeting in July of 2003. It was hot, so we dragged chairs around the elm tree in front of the main house. The main topic was our woods. Forest constitutes half our 40 acres, and is the majority of the land around us. For the first time in many a long year, Bill W led the discussion.

Bill is a man whose natural state might approach part-time hermit status. Generally, ranch meetings give him hives. However, he has lived at the ranch for a very long time. He knows the ditches and the seasonal drainages. He gardens mostly in the nude and produces a huge harvest each year. That July we were still trying to find ways to use the massive quantity of pumpkins stashed over the winter. He wears boots when he gardens, of course. Gardening wearing only boots is not as shocking as splitting wood, which he also does wearing only boots and an axe or chain-saw. Above all, he loves his wife, Lynn, and children, Evan and Zoe, and attends ranch meetings to assure that life is good for them.

Our insurance agent was grumpy about the overgrown state of our forest. Clogged and brushy forest is much more likely to burn and to burn fiercely. Pacific Gas and Electric (PG&E), who provide our electricity, had done an inspection and were concerned about branches and brush too near the electric and phone lines onto our land. Clearly, we had to face up to the state of our trees.

Tom and Bill C offered to trim the branches to meet the immediate PG&E needs, and they completed the job before the weekend was over. Bill W led us on a walk through a part of the forest. Indeed, the floor of the forest was jammed with brush and downed tree limbs. There were several dead trees, likely from the beetle infestation in the drought of a decade ago. The near-100 degree heat of this July day was a reminder that a dry forest is a fire-vulnerable forest.

Roseburg Lumber had circulated a Timber Harvest Plan to log the land that lies immediately to the west of our forest and pasture. We had responded to the Plan with our concerns. We feared the visual impact on our land if logging was done right up to where our pasture fence meets Roseburg land. We were also concerned that Roseburg would apply herbicide in the aftermath of the logging. Herbicide is the cheaper alternative to hand grooming the forest, intended to assure that regrowth is primarily in commercially valuable trees. The Department of Forestry responded to our concerns. First, yes, Roseburg would clear-cut portions of their land, but they would maintain a visual screen between the logged area and our property. We know we live in timber country. At the end of the day, living in a virtual forest is probably better than living in the moonscape of a clear-cut – just barely. Secondly, Roseburg would use herbicide before the cutting and again afterward, but it would be applied on the ground, not aerially, and in the safest possible manner. Apparently, we are in our mother's arms. This is not especially comforting, since the last crew that applied herbicide for Roseburg was made up of non-English-speaking contract workers who had no idea what they were spraying. Neither do we. It was dispiriting to realize that, short of tying ourselves to trees owned by Roseburg Lumber, there was pretty much nothing we could do about the clear-cuts or the herbicide. We committed to hike the next morning through the land destined to be clear cut, from the ranch to Andesite Falls on Hall Creek. It is lovely land, and we determined to enjoy it as it is now.

Bill W had thought through the PG&E issue, as they fussed over brush and fallen timber. More to the point, he had hiked through every corner of the property, often with his teenage son Evan. He knew better than any of us the clogged state of the forest. He proposed that we selectively log our property. We should aim for five goals: protect our land from fire; ensure a healthier forest; open up the views and clear trails; make our insurance folks happier; use any profits for alternative energy development. We struggled, and talked and talked and talked. Some of us still had romantic urban ideas that all logging was violent and possibly avoidable; others dreaded the short term damage big machines would make in the forest. However, one thing that living in this place has taught us all: we need to manage this forest, or fire and tree-falls will do it for us.

We were agreed. We must log, and we must do it soon.

We solicited bids for the work of drafting a timber harvest plan. At the ranch meeting one year later, we selected a forester to do the work. He surveyed the timber and drafted a Timber Harvest Plan. He turned out not to be a perfect choice. It took him forever, and he failed to do a comprehensive survey for endangered species. Likely both of these failings were because he was flummoxed by the notion that every decision on the ranch is made by a group, every tree had to be reviewed, more than half the group were women, and a good number lived far away. We tried to accommodate him. We designated Bill W and Tom to deal with him so that he wouldn't have to lead us all around the woods, especially the girls. But the California Department of Forestry still required a revision of the Timber Harvest Plan, and that, plus the process of sharing the Plan with our neighbors, pushed the project back another year.

Once the Plan was approved, we hired a logger. We were more fortunate in our choice here: Greg has long been a friend, is a lover of the forest, and seemed to have infinite patience for our process. After the forester marked the trees with Greg the first time through, all of us toured the land and identified trees we weren't willing to see logged, and discussed others with Greg. Lynn had specific trees she used for meditation or contemplation by the creek. Evan had trees he had climbed or used as part of the extensive dirt bike trails he built as a middle-schooler. Bill W had the strongest sense that logging must result in safer houses, and was willing to take out any trees that Greg believed needed to go.

The background that Greg provided about this land, and forest management in general, was more important than his specific recommendations. To start with, our forest is all second-growth. Most of the land in this area was logged in the early years of the 20th century. When the forest grows back after logging or fire, trees are often very close together and brush grows throughout as well.

Before these lands were farmed, fire managed the regrowth process. Lightning started many fires; local Indians often used fire to keep the woods open to make hunting easier; even cowboys in the earliest days would start fires behind them when they moved the cows lower on the mountains in the fall. Frequent, low-intensity fires kept the ground open, allowed trees to grow further apart, and eliminated some of the dense brush and low limbs that Greg calls 'ladder fuels.' As all Westerners have learned to their sorrow recently, when this forest management does not happen and when fires inevitably occur, they burn hotter and faster and larger, often so hot that they render the ground unfit for re-growing. Greg is philosophical about this problem in the long run. Mother Nature doesn't care, he says. The land will eventually find a balance and an open and healthy forest will appear. But given the lack of management in the last hundred years, parts of the forest in our neighborhood will not be healthy in any time-line that includes our grandchildren's grandchildren.

With Greg's help, we committed to management of the forest. He identified trees that should be taken out to open up the forest. He also identified trees that should be taken out because they were old or diseased or liable to fall in the foreseeable future. One in particular was a favorite of mine. It had a forked peak, with two trunks poking up in a 'y' shape. Greg said that those 'school-marm trees' are very unstable. "School marm?" I asked. Greg replied, with an actual blush above his heavy red-checked wool coat, that's how she looks with her legs in the air. We discussed each part of the marking of trees in group e-mails and in walks around the forest. It all took considerable time.

The start of logging was delayed another month because so many loggers are also firefighters, including Greg. Most of our crew were out of town on a big Southern California fire. That, of course, was a stark reminder that it was past time for us to be as fire-safe as we could be. Finally, during August and September – two years after we began the discussion – trees fell. Residents became used to the rumble of big machinery down the driveway at dawn. The loggers' water truck, used to keep the dust down and known accurately as 'Mr. Dribble,' was parked semi-permanently in the driveway.

Remarkably quickly, it was done. Many loads of logs were hauled to the mill, with a nice profit to the ranch. These funds have been used to increase our energy independence in these perilous and climate-changing times. There was the bad news: huge piles of slash, waiting for good soaking rains so that they could be burned; no detailed clean-up until after the first winter; big skid trails and logging landings carved into the forest to give access to haul out the logs; a clear view of the neighboring clear-cut from the top of the ridge; the dome house that Fred built sad looking. It had looked cozy tucked under sheltering trees at the edge of the forest. It was now clearly rather small, needed a new roof, and generally looked neglected.

Greg had warned us that the immediate aftermath of logging would be this scarred landscape. But there was also good news: a whole piece of our land was opened up to the potential for rambles, with new views of each of the houses and outbuildings unexpectedly peeking through the trees. Previously, the forest had been explored thoroughly only by mid-sized boys with bikes and adventurers' spirits. The ridge with its clear-cut view now had the potential to become a perfect sled hill. The forest itself seemed to have expanded its shoulders, breathed deeply, and was now ready to welcome in walkers.

The good news has continued in the years following the logging. A fascinating lesson about the impact of trees too close together lies in the vision of a circle of trees around the stump of a large felled tree. Often they lean away from the now empty center, showing how they had to struggle for the light in their earliest years. We have lost a few trees to beetles and now the drought, but in general our forest is much healthier than some in the neighborhood. It remains green and wonderful.

RETIREMENT HOUSE

Bill C and I walk the ranch on the south side of Hall Creek to identify the challenges that need to be solved if we are to build a retirement cabin here. We are aging; our little ranch community is aging. Living together in small spaces and cooking and eating most meals together no longer has the charm it had when we were all young. In fact, I suspect it would not even be tolerable. So Bill C and I initiate the process of building.

It is spring, a lovely time in these foothills. White dogwood blossoms peek through the trees at the forest edge. We imagine a new house in the trees. But summer will come, and with it the threat of fire in the woods. I want to be close enough to the other houses to strengthen and acknowledge that the ranch is a community. Bill wants to be far enough away that he and the other ranchers still feel like we live in the country. That is one difference between a country-raised boy and a city-raised girl. We agree that we want to hear Hall Creek. It has always been a pleasure when we visit to sleep upstairs in the main house with the window open, listening to the creek burble and ripple past the window. Bill is better than I am at considering the realities of infrastructure. We need to be able to extend the electric line and the phone line to any new house. We need to be able to pipe in water from the spring. We must consider how much to extend the driveway, since it is often a challenge to keep it passable in the snow and mud of winter. Can we find a site that meets these physical and emotional requirements?

Bill C and I, of course, bring our life history, ranch history and characters to this decision. Most of all, we bring change into a community that is functioning reasonably well without us as full time neighbors. In addition, residents question whether Bill C and I will be able to cope with life in the country. Long, wonderful, recreational summer days are one thing. Can city slickers live cheerfully with the snow, the mud, the power outages of winter days? When we are old? Can we find a new role here that integrates us with the complex needs of this group of people?

I find the whole process of planning to build difficult. I am not a visual person. I get most of my information from reading, left to right in a linear fashion. I have no confidence that I can figure out what suits me until I have actually lived in the space. What if it is in the wrong place? the wrong shape? too small? too large? too far away from the center of the ranch? I will be moving from the large, rambly 100-year-old house Bill and I have lived in for 30 years. It had extra space for a library, a study, a dining room, a guest bedroom, and a full basement for storage. We married for better or for worse, but not necessarily for 24/7 in a small space. We are aging, entering the years when stairs, maintenance, even cleaning will be more difficult. It turns out that I will make a couple of embarrassing, though not crucial, mistakes in the design of the new house.

Why were we planning to build? Retirement beckoned for me. Some days it loomed. Bill and I always said that when we retired, we would live full time at the ranch for the first time in the thirty years of our ownership. Sharing the land was a decision made years ago when the ranch was organized. That part held no fears. Sharing a garden, a freezer, a lawn mower, a washing machine all seemed sensible and even responsible. But moving into the communal space of the main house wasn't going to happen. The ranch has left the close fellowship of the earliest years behind. Moreover, the main house functions as gathering space for time together and guest space for friends and owners who don't live at the ranch. It houses the community washing machine and dryer and a shared freezer. When people stay there for long periods, the main house no longer feels like shared and comfortable space. If we were to move full time to the ranch, new living space would be required.

The decision about where to build was complicated and took a long time. Bill W and Lynn wanted to be sure that the area around their house maintained its sense of wildness. Bill W is often uneasy with strangers on the property and wanted to be sure that any new driveway not be inviting. Sue is attentive to environmental issues and would monitor our choices of building supplies and energy and water use choices. Sorca's background of relative poverty would fuel a concern that we re-use and conserve where we could in the building process. Tom and Theresa both have a strong sense of design and did not want us to build something that was jarring or of ugly construction. Theresa and Lynn were concerned about whom we would bring onto the property to do the building. The neighborhood is a small one, and the politics are complicated and somewhat mysterious to those of us who haven't lived here full time. Everyone, Bill C and I included, were concerned that we not increase our fire risk or overwhelm our plumbing and energy infrastructure. Any building must protect the integrity of the creek bank. Everyone weighed in as we looked at sites and at building design.

Bill C and I navigated among all these concerns and visions and found the site we believed would work. We did not, of course, come to an immediate decision together. After several tense and sometimes angry discussions, the residents agreed to consider the space. Each time we slammed, or sauntered, or crawled, back into our respective houses. Bill C and I would go back to the main house where we stay when we visit, and where I would stay to supervise the building process. The main house was not our house, it was the community house. We didn't have a house yet.

The site was (and is) near the creek, behind Lynn and Bill W's house. There was a pleasant bowl of space there, ringed with trees. It was newly visible after the logging that took out older, ailing trees and reduced crowding in the forest. So the space had an open feel, stripped of crowded trees and dense blackberry bushes. We strung what looked suspiciously like crime scene tape around the footprint where a house might stand, and the discussion with the other householders began.

We called in our logger friend Greg to tell us how we could be as fire safe as possible. We called in David, who lived at the ranch in the 1970s, knows us all well, and would supervise the building of the house. He, along with Tom, could tell us whether the utilities would work here, the creek bank be stable, and the driveway manageable. Bill and I came to agreement about what the house would look like, including roof lines, so that our ranch-mates could understand what this would mean to our shared space. After a year of debate, anxiety, grumbling, we had a plan and the building began. We committed to consultation about the workers who would come onto the property. Bill C and I knew how challenging the construction project would likely be. We had completed a major remodel of the dining room in our city house in Sacramento after a plumbing catastrophe. It took half again as long as planned. It was enlivened by Bill's constant worrying over the contractor's work. The contractor finally suggested that Bill simply pee on the contractor's tool box. It would then be clear to all of us that the house belonged to Bill. The final clean-up of that project had to be done by a carpenter friend when the contractor's recurring drug problem flared up and he disappeared.

We avoided some of the construction challenge for the ranch project by purchasing a log house from a company in Southern Oregon with a model designed for people with impaired imaginations like me. We picked a general style. The company built the framework of the house under a giant barn in Oregon where we could walk through it. When we approved, they dismantled the house, marked the logs, and trucked it to the ranch. The log house folks supervised a couple of local workers and the house was reassembled like a Lincoln Logs project. Then the electricity, the plumbing, and the internal doors and wall finishing would be done with our local workers.

Building was supervised by our friend David, and the main work done by his son John. John brought in several local helpers over time, skilled at such jobs as roofing, flooring, and finish work. Jimmy, good friend from down the road and an honorary godfather to John, made a chronicle of the building process with his camera, providing a historical record for Bill and me.

The first building mistake concerned the partial second story, a bedroom dubbed the 'grandbaby room'. I remained very concerned about total space. How on earth were we to live in such a small area? When David and John outlined how much of the great room floor space would be taken up by stairs to the grandbaby room, I panicked. "Never mind," I said. "Just put in windows overlooking the great room with swing-out shutters and then put in outdoor stairs on the other side of the room." The builders had already put in the interior wall with two windows when I realized what we were doing. I imagined telling my grandchildren, "If you have to use the bathroom in the night, just go to the far side of the room, walk down the outside stairs, past the mountain lions and brown bears, and come in the front door." John tore out one of the indoor windows, put in a door, and we have a somewhat odd but workable set of indoor stairs.

The second building mistake was in the kitchen. We ordered the cupboards and cabinets from a local cabinet-maker. When he asked what height the cabinets should be, I remembered all the back-aches caused by washing dishes in normal or shorter sinks at my 5'10" height, and told him about how high I thought they should be. I did not factor in the extra couple of inches that would be added by the small pedestal under each cabinet. The result is cabinets with working space too tall for any of my grandchildren, and most of my women friends. So I do the dishes myself.

I reached my limit on one occasion when, after a long search, the electrician I found was rejected, with considerable heat, by Theresa on the grounds that his wife was a jerk. "That's it," I thought. "I can't do this. I can't subject even the smallest decisions to a group discussion. I can't live in a community that requires me to adopt everyone else's prejudices." Bill C talked me down from the ledge and counselled that it was time for a week away from the job of supervising the building. When I considered the possibility of digging up the concrete foundation to the house and starting over someplace else, I simply got over it and found an acceptable electrician.

After nine months of building, we were nearly done. Christmas was coming, and Bill C contributed his own special brand of chaos to the task. "Let's have the annual New Year's Party at our new house. I've invited my brother and his wife to come from Alabama." We had no toilet yet, the electricity wasn't quite done, and the finish carpentry wasn't done either. I spent the month before Christmas shrieking. "If the toilet isn't done, and we have to explain to guests how to use the barrel in the back yard, I'm spending the holidays in a motel by myself with a brandy bottle."

It all mostly came together. It is lovely and livable space. South-facing windows in the great room bring in warmth in the winter when the sun is low, and are shaded in summer by the front porch overhang. The composting toilet works well and doesn't smell. The screened back porch provides a lovely place to eat when it is warm, with the sounds of the creek a grand accompaniment. The space is plenty, even opulent, for two adults. The role we play in the community has developed and seems to work well. My failure to garden enthusiastically seems to be offset by my willingness to be the one who keeps track of the property taxes, the insurance policy, and the registering of water rights. We have dinner together regularly, and are helpful to each other without being intrusive.

SUE AND SORCA'S WEDDING

Four women were gathered in a mini Carrie Nation reunion in June 2013. Gail was visiting from the east coast, so Sue and Sorca and I drove up to Lake Tahoe to spend a few days together. As always, we laughed, caught up on family, and cooked good meals. A flurry of messages lit up our cell phones on June 26. The Supreme Court was preparing to issue their opinion on California's gay marriage law. Gail and I stood in the kitchen in the morning, brewing the first coffee of the day and glued to our cell phones. We had no faith that this particular Court was likely to do the right thing. Then, a miracle: the Court upheld a California appeals court finding that gay marriage was legal under the state constitutional guarantee of equal treatment.

We peeked into Sue and Sorca's bedroom door, where they were still sleeping. "Congratulations"! We sang, "You're getting married in the morning!" Sue and Sorca were wide-eyed, freshly awake, stunned by the knowledge that their relationship could be legal, protected, acknowledged in the civil courts. They smiled and cheered. However, they were not prepared to jump to a declaration. They leaned into each other. Who can know the elements of a decision to marry, or not? Surely, the strength of Sue and Sorca's relationship, which had lasted thirty years, might suggest that they not fix what wasn't broken. Also, both had spent their work lives as professors and were accustomed to examine questions thoroughly before speaking.

The decision could not have been more timely, as Sorca was unwilling to have Sue out of her sight and had been uncharacteristically clinging. The diagnosis of Alzheimer's that was to come was not a complete surprise. Sue and Sorca had lesbian and gay friends who had been denied access to a sick partner in the absence of a legal document. So they mulled over their response to the news.

As soon as they returned home to the ranch, they announced a wedding date. It would be barely a month ahead and would be held at the ranch. It was not to be a big wedding, but it would include all their beloveds.

Family and friends began to gather. Kathie, Sue's oldest friend, would be there and would officiate. Kathie's sister Julie, also a long-time friend, planned to be there and would bring a wedding cake. Sue's step-children from her marriage to Chuck, Chris and Laurie, would attend. Both had spent years of their early adulthood at the ranch. Sorca's daughter Jen would come from the east coast, with her husband Chris and two children, Olive and Arlo. Sorca's second daughter Emilie would be there with her two children, Casey and Sadie.

Houses were scrubbed and polished. Tables and chairs were rented, table cloths from every ranch household rounded up, and good accommodations located for the out-of-town folks. The tables and chairs were set out under the elm tree on the lawn in front of the main house. The food was easy, as everyone who came wanted to participate with some contribution. Salmon and chicken were prepared for grilling. The buffet table in the main house was filled to groaning with salads and vegetables and breads, all prepared with love for the brides. Cases of beer and wine, including champagne for toasting, along with vats of lemonade, were iced.

The day arrived, warm but not as beastly hot as it can get in our part of the world. Sue and Sorca were looking elegant in new clothes, flowing white pants and bright dressy shirts. Indeed, we were all dressed up, a rarity in these mountains. We giggled and whispered as we waited for the wedding party to emerge from Sue and Sorca's little red house to join us under the elm tree.

Kathie stepped forward to conduct the formal part of the ceremony, using words drafted by Sue and Sorca with her help. Kathie is short, dark-haired and animated in most settings. Her hair is now streaked with gray and her glasses sparkled as she looked out over all the friends, family, colleagues gathered to celebrate this wedding. She guided the service gently. She called on all of us to witness the transition from committed soul mates and partners and lovers to a legally recognized family. She talked of the historic importance of ceremony to community. She expressed our shared commitment to the bonds of love and family. Sorca's daughter Jen spoke of the struggles she had as a young teen when her mother told her that Sue was not just a roommate. She spoke of the gifts of integrity, honesty and love in Sue and Sorca's relationship that overcame those struggles. Sorca's younger daughter Emilie spoke of her joy in seeing her mother settling into a strong and loving relationship. Emilie's son Casey, at the complicated age of 13, was a show-stopper. He stepped up before the gathered adults, talked of how important his Granny and Sue-Sue were to him and how happy he was to see this wedding. Sue's stepchildren, Chris and Laurie, were there to support and cheer. Sue's sister Nancy and Sorca's sister Sheila both brought the blessings of birth families to this union. Ranch residents from the past were there as part of the family. Several members of the Carrie Nation gathered to love and honor two of their own.

Dinner was served buffet style, and toasts were made around the circle. Music had been organized by Casey, the first time he had stepped into a lead role in a ranch event. He was proud that he had selected a huge array of music that he was sure Granny and Sue-Sue would like. He was assisted by my granddaughter

Catherine, and it seemed like a part of a family wedding to watch those two 13-year-olds begin to experiment with flirting. Catherine wore Casey's hat and the two spent the dinner looking sidelong at each other.

We toasted the two brides. We told stories of ranch adventures. We toasted those we missed, Fred and Judy especially. We re-told Carrie Nation times together over the years. We even toasted the Supreme Court. All the parts of this wedding day were traditional and replayed weddings over many many years in country front yards where family and friends, adults and children, gathered to celebrate a couple's commitment. It seemed surprising that it had taken such a long time, and legal action at the highest level, for the state to formally recognize what family and community had long seen as a marriage.

CARRIE NATION RE-RISES

Kathie published her book in the fall of 2014, "Take Me To Mercy." The sub-title was "How the Carrie Nation Changed My Life." Kathie was one of the original purchasers of the ranch and a founding member of the women's group, the Carrie Nation Rises. The book contained a disclaimer at the beginning: the work is a piece of fiction. Having said that, much of it is true. So, copies of the book quickly travelled around the circle of Carrie Nation Sisters.

Some of the Sisters Carrie were in regular contact. Others I hadn't seen since the 1970s. As nearly as we could remember, the last time we had gotten together formally was for the service for Molly upon her death in 1995. She had been the oldest member in our early days, a full participant rather than a mentor or mother. In fact, on this reunion occasion, we remembered Molly saying, "None of us had the mothers we deserved." The discussion that prompted this comment was not so much about our own mothers. In the early 1970s, figuring out how to be a woman and a mother, much less a daughter, was confusing and challenging. Expectations had changed; choices had expanded. Most of us worked; many of our mothers did not. Work was a necessity to keep food on the table for most who did work. Pills and diaphragms made sex before, or even outside, marriage much less physically risky than even in our high school years. However, we were all one way or another to discover the emotional risks of so-called 'free love'. Raising children to thrive in this brave new world seemed a monumental hill to climb, with few guideposts from our own families. More fondly, we relished Molly's design of the raft Carrie Nation entered in a spring Sacramento River float in the mid-1970s, powered by a size 156 ZZZ bra-sail and enormous quantities of beer. Her final years had some sad parts: Molly was an architect, so her relationship to the world was visual. Macular degeneration took her sight almost completely. It was a bitter pill, softened somewhat by the support of her beloved husband Allyn. As she always had, Molly's final years showed us another part of the arc of a life.

Kathie's book prompted a heart-warming round of e-mails. Starting with a handful of names in regular contact, we built a list of Sisters who had been members during the 1970s and 80s. Many of the earliest e-mails were questions to Kathie: "Who was Paulette? Did she really have an affair with her boss?" "It's fiction, it's fiction, it's fiction " said Kathie every time. In short order, the talk turned to the possibility of getting together. Could we gather in the spring? Could we gather at the ranch? Debate over timing reminded me of the old days, where everyone needed to have a say and extraneous concerns often took center stage. When would it be too hot for anyone no longer accustomed to valley heat to return to Shasta County? When would the rain that always makes the ranch driveway challenging stop? As it turned out, of course, the rain never came in 2015. We landed on a date at the end of April.

As we gathered, the most notable and least surprising fact was the amount of food and wine and beer that came with each arrival. We had roughly assigned meals to the participants. This, of course, prompted more back-and-forth e-mails. Was anyone still, or newly, vegetarian? What kind of vegetarian? Would anyone be offended if someone's husband sent up his famous chili (it was delicious). If someone's husband's team won the softball tournament, she would have to leave early to see the play-offs and couldn't be there to serve her assigned breakfast. On it went, right up to a couple of days before we gathered. Everyone, it seemed, planned for the likelihood that one of the others would be such a flake that we'd go hungry, or thirsty. I was a part of that problem, shopping with Gail on the day before for dinner the first night and adding lunch makings for every day thereafter, because what if we had no leftovers? As it happened, we spent a huge chunk of each of the three days together in the kitchen of the main house, cleaning up after one incredible feast, then chopping vegetables or watching others chop vegetables, or baking, or assembling main dishes for the next incredible feast. Leftovers were available in great profusion. We drank every bit of that wine and beer, raising the level of laughter, and candor, up a notch with each hour. Those of us who live at the ranch ate leftover food for days afterward.

Of course, we gossiped. Kathie's story was fiction, it really was. However, it turns out that at least two of the staff at the poverty program were indeed sleeping with the boss. We moved through the other poverty program workers, and the legal community where some of our ex-husbands and some of our Sisters worked. We all knew that one of our husbands, at least, was sleeping with his secretary. Several of us slept with colleagues or out-of-town visitors. We knew, to our sorrow, that one Sister slept with the husband of another. Forty years had made that betrayal a thing of the past, at last. From the vantage point of the post-AIDS world, and from our own ages of 60-plus, even 70-plus, it is astonishing to realize how much sleeping around we did, or knew about, or worried about.

We walked, to appreciate the spring that had overtaken these hills, and to prepare for the next extravagant meal. The walking underscored in some part the inevitable indignities of reaching our sixties and seventies. Bobi and Pam had both had serious scares with their hearts, and had worked hard to regain the ability to take a good hike. Gail had taken a bad fall from a horse and had taken months and months to recover. I am struggling not to notice that my left knee is not working well. To be honest, Gail was kind enough to point out that when your body's core sits in your lap for fifty years, it takes a while to rebuild your strength. One of the discoveries of aging is the indignity and the constraints, the inevitability of our biology. Gail and I were the last, the slowest, of the hikers. But then, that was true in our thirties. So we watched Kitty and the other more active athletes move out to conquer the hills, and we covered the ground, but at a leisurely and conversational pace.

We caught up on all the family news. Most of us now have grandchildren, and it was a great pleasure to share stories and pictures. We reported on our children, many of whom we saw birthed or watched through their early years. Most are doing well: happy in their personal lives, working at jobs they find fulfilling or at least pay the rent, and birthing spectacularly adorable grandchildren. When children cause grief, through troubles or mistakes or illnesses, it is harder to talk about and would take more than a couple of days' reunion to restore the trust to do so. But sharing the good parts, and the satisfaction of raising children we like as adults, was a pleasure.

The swapping out of mates seems to have ended at least twenty years ago, although the course of coupled life doesn't always run smoothly. One of our number is fed up with her husband's drinking, but unable to leave a man she loves. Another finds it hard to be away from home for more than a night or two because of the fragility of her husband's health. Yet another finds it hard to accept a husband whose aging leads to a tendency to hunker down at home before she is ready for that phase of life. We talked again of the Carrie Sisters who are no longer with us, Judy and Molly. Molly herself would have looked at us with affection and reminded us that no part of this very human life is easy, smooth, or free of drama.

Work, careers, accomplishments were also a mixed bag, although generally cheerful. More than half of us are now retired, so there was little talk of the daily drama of work, but some sense of adding up our collective achievement. We talked with dismay about the political challenges, even losses in this new millennium. Those like me in the poverty program believed that we could make a substantial impact on poverty and its ravages in family lives, especially for children. Our accomplishment? Poverty rates are probably higher today than they were in the early 1970s when we took on the challenge. Those like Sue and Lee and Kathie that took on racism and civil rights believed that ours was the generation that would see real equality. Our accomplishment? Legal rights have improved some, but recent actions in Missouri, South Carolina, Chicago and elsewhere prove that racism remains alive and well in this country. Especially poignant for Carrie Nation, of course, is that we believed we really achieved the right to determine our reproductive life, in concert with our partners and medical providers. This was especially important for the oldest of us, who grew up before 'the pill' and when back-alley abortions were the only ones available without going out of the country. Our accomplishment? We are watching furious attacks, too often successful, on Planned Parenthood and accessible abortion when chosen. Pam, often the philosopher, reminded us that Mother Theresa advised that "God doesn't require that we fix the problem – just that we try." We can only hope that this is true. We certainly did not make the societal changes we thought we should. Sometimes, the changes we made were not what we expected. We did the best we could.

All of our story-telling about our lives, past and present, was put into sharp focus by the evidence that Sorca's dementia diagnosis was real. She and Sue had taken a wise step: Sorca's daughter came to stay through the weekend of the reunion, providing Sorca with more company of her own. In any case, much of the Carrie Nation history happened before Sorca came into Sue's life. Sorca's worry that her dementia causes those around her to ignore her and treat her like a child was accelerated by a gathering where she had little part in many of the stories that people were telling. By the time two days had passed, she was furious and inclined to take it out on Sue for not being able to include her fully in this gathering of women who talked loudly and laughed more, all around a set of experiences that weren't hers. Sorca's daughter, a gifted therapist, was able to defuse most of the anger and tension. However, it was a sad and sobering discovery, a reminder that this is our time of life. We face growing disability, physical and mental, for ourselves and for those we love. We face challenges in the task of assuring that the life that remains is as full and warm and fulfilling as we can make it. Perhaps more importantly, family and long-time friends provide the support and love that will get us through this time of life with grace.

Chapter 3
Growing Land

I am interested in the way that a man looks at a given landscape and takes possession of it in his blood and brain. For this happens, I am certain, in the ordinary motion of life. None of us lives apart from the land entirely, such an isolation is unimaginable. We have sooner or later to come to terms with the world around us – and I mean especially the physical world, not only as it is revealed to us immediately through our senses, but also as it is perceived more truly in the long turn of seasons and of years.

N. Scott Momaday, from *An American Land Ethic*, as quoted in *Bedrock: Writers on the Wonders of Geology*, ed. LE Savoy, EM Moores and JE Moores.

Eastward Shasta extends beyond the curving Sierra range into the alkali and sage-brush plains of Lassen. This forbidding feature, together with hostile Indians, operated against settlement in this county, and the early immigrants who skirted the western end saw no inducements even in Shasta. Besides the trappers, Fremont, Greenwood and other explorers may have skirted Lassen county. Lassen passed through it in opening the Pit River route of 1848.

History of California, Vol. VI. 1848-1859. Hubert Howe Bancroft, 1888, p. 493

Big Wheels Ranch lies on the west side of the Cascade mountain range in Northern California, roughly midway between the Shasta and Lassen peaks. The ranch itself is about 3000 feet in elevation. Hatchet Pass over the Cascades to the east is a bit more than 4300 feet. We benefit from our location on the west side of the range, catching considerably more rain than the high desert plateau to our east. Our climate is described as Mediterranean. We are affected by drought from time to time, along with the rest of California. We also have the occasional El Nino year with quantities of rain. We have some snow virtually every winter, though it rarely stays on the ground for long periods.

We are in forest land, dominated by ponderosa pine and Douglas fir. Cedar, oak and maple trees are present, and the dogwood provides a spectacular fall display each year. The understory is often clogged with ceanothus and, at the disturbed edges, blackberry. Virtually all the surrounding forest is second growth, reflecting the logging that was the main activity here at the end of the 19th century and the beginning of the 20th.

The communities nearby are not incorporated and are very small indeed. Montgomery Creek, where we get our mail, has a population of less than 200. The aforementioned post office, a small convenience store run by the Pit River tribal government, an elementary school, and a small café are the total of the commercial opportunities. In the larger area, including Round Mountain, a health clinic, fire station, equipment rental company, small garden store, community center, cemetery, and another elementary school are the nearby services. The small city of Redding is 45 miles away and is the service center for a large part of far northern California. The town of Burney, with a few restaurants, hardware store, grocery store and a broader collection of business establishments is about 10 miles away. Shopping requires transportation for the most part, though on-line service has changed some elements of life, including access to a real newspaper and it provides a substitute for lack of a bookstore. The power goes out a couple of times every year due to snow, heavy rain or wind, or some doofus driving over what I imagine is a very small line connecting us to the outside world. In short, we are legitimately rural, with all the joys and the challenges that entails.

Finally, like most of rural America the politics locally are conservative. Many of our neighbors are off-the-grid folks who don't trust much of any level of government. Our local elected officials range from extremely conservative to old-school Republican. On the other hand, folks from all points on the anarchist to socialist spectrum believe that neighbors are neighbors and generally reach out to help each other when it is time to evacuate ahead of a fire, shovel/plow the snow, or simply get to the post office. We've had our share of meth-cookers at the worst of times, and the populace is pretty well-armed, but all in all folks who live in the area are encouragingly respectful of differences.

LIONS, OH MY!

Bill W and Lynn woke one winter morning at the ranch to find that a mountain lion had killed one of the goats from the pen next to the house they shared with Evan, 8, and Zoe, 6. Bill and Lynn were too old to be hippies anymore, but both have a gentle connection to the earth, and to this land in particular. However, they had a fierce response to the killing of the goat. The lion killed with a single, surgical cut down the belly, ate only the heart and liver and covered the rest with leaves, saving it for another nocturnal visit. The kill was all the more shocking, as the goat was roughly the size of 8-year-old Evan.

The state of California has an initiative-passed law intending to conserve the mountain lion, so there is a procedure for dealing with mountain lion kills. Bill called the California Department of Fish and Game, whose local representative was a stocky combination of ranger-enforcer and local county boy. He explained that you had your 'predating' lions: ones that took livestock close to houses, for example. These were different from your 'public safety' lion: those that took livestock next to a school, or actually threatened a person. Bill was issued a permit to kill a 'predating' lion, as long as he killed it within 72 hours and called Fish and Game immediately to pick up the carcass.

So Bill and Lynn, who hadn't fired a shot in years, crouched outside the next night in the cold, near the dead goat. The goat was fixed with bells, and they waited for the lion to return. When it came, they fired and missed, eight times in all. The lion was faster than Lynn could train the flashlight so Bill could focus in the dark. There was menace in how the lion skipped to the tree-line after a shot, but didn't leave. It waited for the inevitable relaxation of the hunters. When the lion returned near dawn, they finally managed to synchronize the flashlight and the gun. It was done: the lion was dead.

Bill and Lynn, and the children, fell into a relieved sleep. Just as the sun came up, like a returning nightmare or ghost, the bells on the dead goat jingled again. Lynn feared the dogs might have gotten into the pen and rushed to look. A second, larger lion fled her flashlight. Bill and Lynn were frantic.

By daylight, it was clear the lion Bill shot was young, probably a yearling. The larger lion was doubtless Mom, and she would be back. The Fish and Game ranger stood for a long time with his field boot on the bumper of his pickup, speculating that this pair was likely responsible for taking out 8 goats from down the road. If true, this lion pair had wiped out the stock of one small farmer. And our small farmers were tired and spooked at the thought of their children being out of sight. In fact, all the residents and members of the ranch were spooked: probably every one of us had voted for that Mountain Lion Conservation Act, and every one of us was caught by the menace to home and family.

Bill called a pair of experienced local hunters, brothers who grew up in these hills and who were on the Fish and Game's 'approved' list. They were officially authorized by the State to use their hunting dogs to tree and kill that predating lion. And so they came at the next dawn, after another long night of bell-tinkling visits by the lion. It was over in 20 minutes. The lion was still so close to the house that the dogs treed her immediately and she was a clear shot for the fatigue-clad brothers. She died suddenly, cornered and slain, a daylight anti-climax to what had become a nightmare.

The lion was beautiful, a sleek 80-pound, 6-foot muscle from nose to tail tip, tawny even in death, huge feet with claws whose surgical precision we had seen in the goat. She lay in the driveway for the couple of hours it took for the Fish and Game ranger to come and certify the kill and take the lion. He had been formal and full of his 'predating' forms the day before, determined that any shooting be within the state's guidelines. But he put chains on his truck that Sunday morning and slogged over the pass from headquarters to certify the kill and talk us all through the aftermath of a killing.

Eight-year old Evan knelt by the lion. He is a tow-headed boy, wiry and every bit as comfortable in the forest as his father. He picked up the lion's head, and roared his loudest African lion-roar at this lion's fangs. He moved away to play, came back to push out the claws from her padded feet, and roared again. He was coming home, it seemed, assuring himself that he could feel strong and safe here again.

Those hunting brothers were something, too. After the kill, the two hunters came in for coffee and Lynn's fresh cinnamon rolls.

Lean and comfortable, they propped their big rifles by the door. They knew the historic range of lions and said that lions had become more accustomed to people. The lion numbers in our neighborhood had also been affected by the large local fire some years ago. The replacement of trees with brush, at least temporarily, had increased the deer, increasing the lions in response. When the Ranch ducks came by for breakfast, one brother remarked, "You're runnin' a full-service cougar deli here, aren't you? Snacks as well as full-goat meals." They believed the lions would have kept coming back until all the ranch animals were gone, eating only the best parts, the innards, at first. They believed that the two house cats and one dog missing from here over the last year had fed the lions. 'House cats are a favorite,' they said, 'and horses too. Cougars are at the top of the food chain; they take what they want.' Bill W confessed that when one of the ranch neighbors lost stock, he thought it wouldn't happen to us. "Our vibrations are better." Once a hippie, always a hippie, it seems. Bill went on to say, "Excuse me. I'm embarrassed that I need to say this….but I do. He's an expert, he brought his brother and his dogs, the lion was treed 20 feet away and in daylight, and he got his lion. I'm not an expert, I had no brother and no dogs, it was dark, the lion was moving, and I got my lion."

WATER

When Demetria came back to the ranch for the first time in 20-some years, she had a list. She had lived here as a young girl with her parents. She brought her husband, a country boy from Cuba who was delighted to be out of the city, and their two young children. She loved staying in the main house, with its familiar logs and living room gathering place. The toys in the upstairs room felt familiar, even if they weren't the same she had while here. She was astonished at the additions to Lynn and Bill's house, which had been her parents' house when she was a baby. The chickens couldn't possibly be the same ones scratching in the dirt near the garden, but they could be related. Mostly, however, Demetria wanted to walk the creek and find the watercress and mint. She wanted to visit the waterfall on Hatchet Creek, a favorite of local teens who risk at least limb if not life jumping into the pool. She wanted to go down to the Pit River, visiting the natural hot springs and dipping into the river itself.

Water: it is our life and our delight. We drink it, of course. I start most days in a bathtub with bubbles. We listen to it from all our houses, burbling along in Hall Creek. We keep our hundred-year-old apple trees alive and producing, and grow vegetables every summer. The pond in the back pasture provides cool dips in the summer. All of our young grandchildren have learned how to paddle a canoe on this protected water. The pond is home to overwintering Canada geese. Water is at the center of this ranch and of this landscape.

Every summer for many years, we would gather over the 4th of July at a spot on the Pit River called Sand Rock. Ed and Ray's ranch is a 14-mile trip north and down a bit to the level of the Pit River coursing from these mountains to join the Sacramento river. They are close neighbors in this rural area. From their ranch house, a short but terrifying path leads down a steep bank to the river to the large flat sandstone rock. Indeed, Sorca's youngest daughter brought one daring boyfriend up in her early twenties and he broke his ankle sliding on the steepest part of the path to the river. Except for that dramatic occasion, every year we somehow managed to get adults and children and quantities of picnic food down to the water's edge. We all would climb into the river upstream of the rock and float and whoop down to the sand rock. Many years we would haul inner tubes down and float all the way from Sand Rock to the bridge in the hamlet of Big Bend. I can't imagine now entrusting my grandchildren to the fast-moving and rock-strewn current. Somehow, no one bashed their head or got stuck up against a rock. Something must protect fools and river lovers.

Our particular water basin is that of the Pit River. The Pit is one of only three rivers that cross the Cascade mountain range (the others are the Columbia and the Klamath). It is really the major source of the Sacramento River, providing as much as 80% of the water that forms Shasta Lake above Redding. The 200-mile-plus length of the river winds mostly through the high volcanic desert areas east of the Cascades, draining old and crystal clear volcanic springs and snow from the Cascades. Our Hall Creek falls into the Pit below Big Bend. Although we see lower water because of this most recent drought, the Pit River flows well year-round and so does Hall Creek that runs through our ranch. The Pit waters two-thirds of the producing crops in the county: grain, truck crops, rice, strawberries, horseradish, garlic, and peppermint.

Historically, the Pit River provided abundant resources of salmon, most importantly Chinook or King Salmon. These elegant and iconic creatures live most of their lives in the ocean. However, they are born in flowing streams, from eggs deposited and fertilized by their parents as a last act before dying. The young salmon spend a few months growing and then move downriver to the ocean. Ultimately, they move back into fresh water, following some internal compass back to the stream where they were born, to repeat the cycle of spawning. Salmon, joyfully leaping up rapids and through calm water, supported local people for thousands of years and delighted European newcomers to the area. Sadly, salmon no longer swim the Pit River. Shasta Dam blocked passage to the Pit in the late 1930s; salmon today are captured at Keswick Dam downstream from Shasta Dam and are trucked to a local fish hatchery. Warm water and reduced gravel downstream from dams have further damaged salmon habitat. There are efforts throughout the north state to identify ways to restore natural salmon runs. However, no serious proposals have been made to eliminate Shasta Dam. As beautiful as they were when they graced our rivers and streams, salmon are unlikely to return to this part of the world any time soon.

Although our visions of Hall Creek and the Pit River are this year dominated by drought, we also remember that the Pit and its tributaries can be fierce and threatening. In the late 1990s, we experienced a New Year's flood of major proportions. Bill C and I drove down to Big Bend to see how bad the flood might be. The Pit River was turbulent, flooded, powerful, loud. From the bridge in Big Bend, we could hear the grinding, thunderous sound of Volkswagen Beetle-sized boulders rolled by the river. I could feel the rumble inside my belly as I heard it in the bridge timbers. There was land-changing power in the river.

I wanted to go across the bridge to see the remains of the Nelson Creek bridge, torn out by a giant log and stranding Ed and Ray at their ranch. But curtains of rain were intimidating and we couldn't see the edge of the road. So we settled instead for weak, acid-tasting coffee at the Pit Stop convenience store on the near side of the bridge. The bad coffee was more than offset by the hot news from a numbed PG&E lineman, smelling like every minute of his 18-hour shift in a dripping poncho, trying desperately to keep the power on. "The Nelson Creek bridge is gone, eating a road grader in the process," he said. Little Roaring Creek was undercutting the road between Big Bend and our ranch. It could go at any time. "Go home," he said. "It's fixin' to get worse."

The storm worsened on New Year's Day and the next. As it did, the footbridge over Hall creek between the main house and the meadow tilted, then was pulled away by the power of the water. Fat domestic ducks and geese lived in the meadow at the time. How could they get across the creek for the morning feed? None of us had ever seen them fly. The culvert under the road filled up, creating a waist-high stream for a while that cut off the road and diverted a stream down the driveway, threatening the dome house. On the one hand, it was a 'Boy's Life' kind of disaster for us. We all piled out into the warm rain to gather rocks and bricks, building a berm across the driveway to keep the dome dry for another night.

On the other hand, what would happen next? I found myself worrying and fussing. I found I really could wring my hands. The ducks would go hungry, the road was under water, half the road-clearing equipment in the eastern part of the county was listing into Nelson Creek, and the lights and phone were out, in spite of the best efforts of that weary lineman. As my worry increased, I thought I needed that phone. I proposed getting into the car again, going down the road to see if the bridge had gone and whether we were marooned. I thought about calling my son, my mother, someone to talk to about this disaster. Bill C grabbed me by the shoulders. "Calm down. We have a wood stove, plenty of dry firewood, enough food to last for weeks, and plenty of wine. The only way you could get into real trouble is to keep flapping your arms and try to go someplace." He was right. We were fine. It was time to make soup.

Finally, after three harrowing days, the power was restored – cheers to our lineman. The dome stayed dry – cheers to our berm builders. The driveway needed some re-grading. The ducks and geese fussed and chattered, then flapped across Hall Creek to join us for lunch. The soup was better on the second day – it always is.

When Bill and I drove back to our city life, we drove past the desolate sight of families downstream, picking through a lifetime of treasures flung across the canyon by furious raging tributaries to the Pit River. Whatever our own anxiety and concern, we were reminded of our luck, and the blessing of living upstream.

FIRE

It is summertime as I write these words, and we are worried about fire. Every summer we worry about fire, from May until the first solid rain in the fall. We scan the sky for any signs of smoke. We follow closely planes and helicopters in the sky: are they spotting for fires? We check the news every night and the CalFIRE web site often. CalFIRE is the state agency that provides fire protection on private lands and for areas like ours that don't have their own fire department. We live not at the forest edge, but actually in the forest. We know that fire is a regular part of the cycle of these mountains. We know that fire nearby is inevitable: the questions are when, and what will we lose when it comes.

In these globally warming days, it also seems hotter than usual – nearing and sometimes reaching triple digits on many days, even at our 3000' elevation. Our intensively insulated homes in normal times hold the heat in winter and retain the nighttime cool in daytime during the summer. That cool barely lasts these days.

We have resisted watering the open areas around our house in this drought year, so the grasses are mostly dry and brown these days. We do continue to water the nearly 100-year-old apple orchard, the small area of more recently planted fruit trees and berry bushes and, of course, the vegetable garden. But the lush green that usually characterizes our woods has dimmed, even browned. Some of the pines are showing signs of beetle damage. The redbud is starting to show autumn colors before the autumn cool down even begins. These changes make the forest seem even more vulnerable to fire.

Set off by summer lightning storms, there are now three fires burning to the east of us, as yet uncontained after two full days of firefighting. Rural neighborhoods have been evacuated, highways closed, and the sky is filled with smoke. The fires are over the crest of the hill and are unlikely to be a direct threat to us. But they raise our fears and worries to a high point.

Each time anyone in the neighborhood smells smoke, we remember the Fountain Fire in August of 1992. Although only Lynn and Bill W and their two children were at the ranch that day, it is the fire that haunts all of us. It started near an old stone water fountain along the highway, ten miles west and south of the ranch. Within eight days it had burned almost 64,000 acres of forest, orchards and buildings. It roared through the communities of Round Mountain and Montgomery Creek and went on to the outskirts of Burney over the crest of the Cascades at Hatchet Mountain. More than 300 homes and nearly 500 additional structures were destroyed.

Lynn and Bill W were at home at Big Wheels that day. At the time of the fire, their oldest child, Evan, was 5 years old and visiting Janet, a potter who had moved recently from the ranch and was living near the spot where the fire started. Bill had gone briefly to check on the group home in Montgomery Creek that he and Lynn supervised. Lynn was home with 18-month-old Zoe, who was napping. Janet, keeping low-key and calm, called Lynn to let her know there was smoke nearby and perhaps Lynn should come pick up Evan. Not overly alarmed, Lynn waited a half hour, hoping Zoe would wake. Finally, she picked up the sleeping toddler and travelled down the highway to gather Evan. In the time since Janet's call, the fire had exploded, filling the sky with smoke. The convenience store near Janet's house had 50-75 worried people standing in the parking lot where Lynn turned to reach Janet's house. Were they evacuees? Watchers?

Sheriffs blocked the lane to Janet's house. Lynn went immediately into mama-brown-bear mode. Her son was on the other side of the barricade and she was going to pick him up. The sheriffs were out-matched and allowed her to pass with the now quiet Zoe. Speeding down the road with tall trees in flames on both sides, Lynn met Janet on her way out. Janet was evacuating with whatever she could pack into her car. She told Lynn that she had already moved Evan to the parking lot of the convenience store. Lynn reversed direction and found Evan among the crowd of folks, now grown to nearly 200. Most of these people, like Janet, had evacuated from roads off the highway and were trying to figure out what to do next. Evan was sobbing, frightened and saying over and over, "The trees are burning, I'm sad for the trees, the trees are burning."

Lynn took the children back to the ranch, where Bill returned shortly. For the moment at least, the family was safe and together. Bill went quickly and quietly to work laying out all the sprinklers to wet the land around the buildings. Then the power went out. With no electricity, there was no pump to drive the sprinklers. To complicate matters, a staff member arrived at the ranch with six boys currently living at the group home. The boys were upset and acting out. They were young teen foster children, each of whom was too troubled to be placed in a regular foster home; each had faced losing a home before, often many times.

Soon, smoke could be seen from the ranch. Without power, it would be impossible to keep the family or the group home boys safe. It was clear that they all needed to leave. Lynn and Bill packed up, taking their computer (rare and expensive in those days), family pictures and sleeping bags and food for a few days. Bill, operating in what Lynn describes as masculine survival mode, made all the physical preparations to keep his family safe. Lynn herself moved from family member to group home boy to family member to be sure everyone was also feeling safe.

They went to stay with friends in Big Bend, 15 miles further east and north. Their friends' house was small, and other friends and neighbors had also fled there for refuge. All the family, including the group home boys, slept in the pasture. By morning they could see the smoke from Big Bend; they could even see the flames when propane tanks exploded in Montgomery Creek, twenty-five miles away. By mid-morning, the order came to evacuate Big Bend.

The next two days are a blur. The group home staffer took three of the boys and traveled north. Bill and Lynn traveled east by narrow, rutted dirt back roads to the state park in Burney, with their children and the remaining three group home boys. There was so much smoke that it was like a winter drive through the fog. The family celebrated one of the group home boys' birthdays with snack cakes from the park store and little candles, in an effort to reassure everyone that life would be normal again. But, before they could sleep, the evacuation order for the park arrived. By now, Lynn and Bill assumed that the ranch was burned; it seemed that the whole of the northern California world was burning. They moved into cramped motel rooms in Redding, after a long drive around the fire.

Four days after the fire started, they came back up the road to Big Wheels, past acres of burned trees and several house foundations. In this rural area, every burned house had belonged to known friends or neighbors. The group home was burned and so was the health clinic where Lynn worked. Ground fires were burning in several places on both sides of the road. Then, the Big Wheels miracle: there was a fire engine in the driveway, the remains of a dump of fire suppressant chemicals at the top of the driveway, and two firemen on watch to be sure that the fires did not reignite in areas beyond the burned ground. The fire had been stopped virtually at our property line. One of those firemen, a Native American, spent some of his hours on watch chipping an obsidian blade for a spear that still hangs in Lynn and Bill's house as a talisman to protect from fire. There was still no power (in fact, there was to be no public power for six weeks), and the smoke and fires along the hill across the road made the ranch unlivable. Bill and Lynn moved into a friends' home down the road. Bill purchased a gas generator and they were able to move back into the ranch by the second week after the fire. The foster care bureaucracy responded helpfully and moved the boys into a temporary group home nearby. Three months later, their group home in Montgomery Creek was rebuilt. Reconstruction of the health clinic took an additional three months.

The aftermath of the fire has been lasting. Evan says that he doesn't exactly remember the event, but that fire during his childhood always made him nervous. He is a strong and capable 20-something, at home in the woods and leading rafting and back-packing trips. It is hard to imagine him nervous about anything. Lynn says that he got counselling for trauma after the event, as even campfires made him panic for years afterward. Lynn and Bill both are hyper-vigilant when there is smoke, or rumors of smoke, in the area.

We have a generator, and gas-fired stream pumps that don't depend on electricity and that can spray areas near our houses when needed. Bill checks them regularly and provides each of us with directions on how to use them. We have cleared defensible space to 50 – 100 feet around all the houses. Every household keeps a list of what to take in the event of evacuation, and we are all familiar with the largely dirt road alternate routes to leaving in the event of evacuation. We keep our insurance policies up to date and hope they don't just decide to cancel as the fire situation worsens.

Analyses of the Fountain Fire have not definitively identified a cause: arson or a spark from a motor of some kind. Regardless, the speed and destructiveness of the fire were aided by the fact that it came at the end of a six-year drought. The weather was exceptionally hot and dry, with no rain for a couple of months. Terrain with a laddering of grass, brush, small trees, and larger trees, provided a perfect fuel on a hot, dry, and windy day.

How about these fires on the horizon today? Drought? Check. No rain? Check. Very hot, dry days? Check. A friend in Burney, who has had to evacuate because of the nearness of his home to the fire lines, said he felt like we were not living in a forest any more, but rather in a tinderbox. We continue to watch the horizon for smoke, check the CalFIRE web site frequently, and flinch whenever helicopters fly over, fearing they are fire-spotting. Wish it would rain.

SNAKES

Snakes are a part of our Ranch landscape: garter snakes, little rosy boas and, of course, rattlesnakes. I don't like them. Indeed, I have a visceral reaction to even their possibility.

My first job in my teens was day-camp counselor. Our director told us we must hold the garter snake to reassure the campers. When I held the snake, it stuck its tail up under the shirt I was wearing and I flung the snake to the ground. The director told me the exact value of the snake (implying that it was higher than the value of a teenage camp counsellor). I was forbidden to touch it again. For the rest of the summer, I had to clean skunk poop off the wire cage where the terrified skunk lived, poked at by dozens of 10-year-olds all day long. I thought I was lucky to still have a job.

When my first child was 6-months-old I was stuck in a crappy little house on the edge of town. That summer, my first husband was gone for weeks at the bedside of his dying father. I came home from the Laundromat one day to find a nearly unreadable note from the garbage man. It was tacked to the back door and a very long rattlesnake was stretched out on the step. It was dead. The note said, 'Kilt her – a Mom. Watch for babies.'

I was terrified. I put baby Ben in his crib, climbed onto the picnic table in the kitchen and began phoning. The sheriff's office laughed. The animal control officer said they didn't do house calls for dead snakes. I had just enough sense not to call my grieving husband 300 miles away. I called the local pest control company. "Lady, we don't do snakes…we do insects…and we do stenches."

I started to cry. "I'm up here with a baby. My beloved father-in-law is dying. I hate this crappy little house on this dry hill. And now I'm surrounded by rattlesnakes." After a long pause, he said, "Do you have a beer? Pour yourself one and I'll be right there."

He drove up in a van with a giant cockroach on the roof. He poked all over the house and the yard and the basement with its door on the downhill side. He came back up and asked for a pie pan. He was gone for a little bit, then came up and said he was ready to leave. "Now, don't you worry. I can't find any snakes. But I've built a snake trap. I've put a pan of water in the basement in the middle of a six-foot wide circle of blue pesticide. If there is a snake within a quarter mile it will come to the water. If it's a little snake, the pesticide will kill it. If it's a big snake, you'll see the tracks. Here's my phone number. Call me any time."

I knew it was bullshit. Still, every day for weeks I checked the snake trap. When I found no tracks, I knew I was okay, and so was baby Ben, for another day.

Now I have grandchildren visiting me in the mountains. I know there are rattlesnakes here, but honestly, I've only ever seen a couple; Tom has killed at least two over the last few years that were close to the houses. I know that the dogs keep the snakes away, generally. But I can barely keep myself from warning Johnny, age 5, and Lizzie, age 7, every time they go outside: don't ever step over a log without looking first, don't stick those hands under rocks, listen carefully, and freeze if you hear the buzz. If I scare them, they won't want to come back. I think maybe I will build myself a snake trap.

One Year's Round of Seasons

Winter

It is wintertime at the ranch. For people who live in areas with more traditional tree cover, the change here may not seem dramatic. The pines and cedar remain vivid green, after all. But the underbrush has mostly died back, in many cases after a dramatic red and gold fall blaze of glory. The aspen trees planted by Fred on the edge of the apple orchard stand stark and white, like lookouts posted to watch for spring. I suppose it is more accurate to say the aspen tree stands watch, since the circle of trees are clones that have grown up from the original aspen. The flowers and ferns around the house have died back. The containers of flowers in front of the house are looking forlorn, but I can't quite face emptying the containers of annuals until the very last green leaf has died. Maybe a New Year's Day project is called for.

The apple trees are even sadder than usual this winter. The apples and the leaves are all gone of course. What is left is an array of many broken branches. This year, bears aggressively raided the orchard. They moved past the windfall apples and low hanging fruit that is their usual tax, and climbed up into the trees. We suspect that the multi-year drought may have made the bears hungrier as winter approached, although we have no real information as to why this year's raids were worse than usual. The disappearance of low apples and little piles of bear poop with seeds and stems inside are as bad as it gets in most years. We'd hate to think that big fences would be needed around the orchard as well as the garden. This is a very old orchard, and the trees really can't handle this sort of attack.

The woods are quiet this time of year. The bears have moved or denned up. The deer, or at least most of them, seem to have moved lower on the mountain as well. Rabbits venture out sometimes.

Winter birds are here: red-shafted flickers and Stellar jays are eager for seed in the feeders. Hummingbirds surprise us by remaining here in the cold, although it is a struggle to provide syrup that isn't frozen solid. Juncos flock and chatter under our porch. The occasional chickadee and nuthatch can be seen as well by the sharp-eyed, and we saw a Mountain Bluebird this morning. Ravens, who are familiar and always a little grumpy, call when the flickers get too close.

The big news this year is that, for the first time in three years, we had decent rains in December. We are a bit ahead of the 'average' rainfall for this time of year, all to the good. It will take much, much more to refill reservoirs and begin to restore the health of beetle-damaged stretches of forest. We have not had more than a trace of snow, but Mt. Shasta to our north is at last draped in winter white, and Mt. Lassen to our south has had enough to close the road through the national park. So much of California's water comes from snow that melts through the late spring and summer that we can only hope for more and more. For now, even this 'average' rainfall seems like a blessing after the dry years.

One impact of a heavy storm coming after years of drought is the falling of trees. In the town of Burney to our east, dozens and dozens of trees fell in the biggest wind storm, crushing cars and lawn furniture and landscaping, blocking roads, but miraculously not killing anyone. The wind was not as devastating on our side of the mountain, but an enormous pine tree fell nearby, more than 100 feet tall. It fell parallel to our house, but it is a reminder that living at the forest edge has its dangers as well as delights. The tree was a 'school-marm' tree, with a forked peak, two trunks poking up in a 'y' shape. One of the forks had been knocked off earlier and, in any case, such trees are unstable at any time, according to our logger friends.

Hall Creek, a small but year-round creek that meanders through our property, is running more fully than it has in months and months, providing a welcome chuckling sound to each of our houses. The Spring Creek Ditch that joins Hall Creek on our property is also more full and cheerful. Neither of these water sources has run dry in our 40-plus years, but in the periodic droughts, they slow down and the spring where we get our water dries up. When it does, we must switch to the ditch, with more mud and debris. A dry spring always creates a concern about the future.

So like bears, we settle in to winter activities in our log cabin cave: correspondence to friends and family to celebrate the holiday, experimenting with soup and stew recipes, a good start on that stack of books next to the bed.

SPRING

Spring came early to the ranch this year, a mixed blessing. After an encouraging spell of rain before Christmas, the rest of winter was resolutely dry and warm. We had virtually no snow, just a dusting on a couple of occasions. It looks like the drought in California will extend to a fourth year. So we face spectacularly beautiful days and moderate temperatures with pleasure and a background sense of dread. We will pay for these days, in dry forests, increased fire danger, and concern for water supplies.

Daffodils are always the first signs of spring, bright yellow flags around most houses and in some older landscapes where earlier settlers planted bulbs. The daffodils are followed shortly by Western Redbud along the roadways. Magenta and purple blossoms flower in bushes that can be as tall as 20 feet and are found on steep slopes. Redbud is a drought tolerant plant, which may be why this year has seen such abundant flowering. The stems of the plant, when young, are a deep red and were used by local Indians in basketry. One of the benefits of the regular burning that local tribes did in the forest was to encourage the growth of young redbud bushes for that purpose. We also find bright yellow forsythia early in the season along roadways. This is not a native plant, and it may have been imported for its bright display early in spring, or for its medicinal uses to treat fever, flu or inflammations. As the redbud begins to fade, the bright white flowers of dogwood bloom. They are an understory tree in our forest, and usually have very good years after logging or other disturbance. Many of the younger dogwood trees are willowy, leaning, with very slim trunks, even though they can grow quite tall. We have been trying to persuade a dogwood behind our house not to bend completely over into the creek, tying it to a nearby pine. Dogwood are even more spectacular in the fall when they turn a brilliant red.

The birds are active in this warm weather. The Anna's hummingbird males have developed their neon red chin vest, and the consumption of sugar-water in our feeder has leaped to new levels. The male hummingbirds are territorial and buzz us when we come close to the feeder.

A Stellar jay family has built a nest in the eaves on our screened back porch. Three young have emerged and they are fed by both parents. The nest was also used last year and the year before. We'd like to believe that the nest is used by the same faithful couple, but who is to know? They seem unbothered by our closeness. Indeed, it seems to me that jays are bothered by very little. They are loud and often seem to be screeching at other birds. They do not migrate, which may give them the right to yell at the climate wimps.

We have begun mowing early in this drought year, struggling to maintain the 100-foot cleared area around the house. We had to call in a logger to fell an enormous fir tree right next to the house that died quickly, apparently from a beetle infestation. The beetles are always with us, we are told. The trees do fine at withstanding them, unless the trees are stressed by drought. The logger came to look at the tree. He came the next day saying he woke worried in the night. A strong wind, he said, would bring the tree down and it was aimed right for the house.

So we move toward summer, astonishingly early this year and with some fear that the dead fir may be only the first casualty to the continuing drought.

SUMMER

I have had nightmares about the deep, wide network of blackberry roots under this ranch, lurking, growing, waiting to wrap around my ankles or my grandchildren. The vines smile at my trivial efforts to eliminate the above-ground traces. A single blackberry cane can develop into a thicket six square yards in size in two years, so slowing them is not trivial. But eradication? I'm not sure I am making any progress.

We don't use herbicides or pesticides, so that is out. I have tried pulling them up: it is slow and hard on the back. We have mowed them regularly: slows them down but does nothing to eliminate them. I am currently using a tool called the 'Weasel Weed Popper' that allows me to twist them up with a few inches of root and does not require me to bend down for each plant.

These plants are Himalayan blackberry. They are native to Armenia and Iran. They propagate from 'nodes', underground buds that grow off established roots. They were introduced to North America in the late 19th century by Luther Burbank because the berries are so large and sweet. They spread rapidly, especially in disturbed areas like the edges of the land where we logged or the perimeter of our house-building site.

Despite my whining, the blackberries do provide a spectacular mid-summer treat. Grandchildren Lizzie and John spent a week here at Grandma and Grandpa Camp camp. They collected more than enough blackberries, plump and beautiful, to make a lovely crisp. When served warm with vanilla ice cream, this dessert makes picking around the thorns worth it. Even so, I still am not sure that any dessert is worth the persistent, garden-clogging growth of these tenacious plants.

There are more welcome summertime plants, of course. The flowers especially are a pleasure early, before the brutal heat of real summer in these parts. Daisies grow abundantly in fields and pastures, blooming in June and July. These are also apparently an introduced plant, the Ox-eye daisy. Luther Burbank hybridized them to produce the larger Shasta daisy for home gardens, named for the snows of our mountain. We have lots of Ceanothus, sometimes called California lilac. They are native, and deer love their blue-purple clusters of tiny flowers. They grow so well in our area, however, that they provide a brushy understory that is threatening in the event of fire. We are committed to the removal of some of the Ceanothus in the forest edges, to open up the area and to reduce what our fire-fighting friends call 'ladder fuels.' As July arrives, the bright blue daisy-like flowers of chicory blossom. This plant is also a favorite of deer. I should try drying chicory roots and mixing it with coffee, in memory of depression and war-era fillers or substitutes for expensive and hard-to-find coffee. Perhaps this summer.

We've had a little rain in early July, very unusual. Weather experts increasingly speculate that we might be looking at an El Nino winter, with the warmer ocean waters possibly bringing in more rain than usual. In order to truly banish the drought, we would need much more rain as well as snow to keep the water flowing later in the year. We can only hope.

I announced firmly when we moved full- time to the ranch that no one should be thinking that I will turn into a farmer or even a gardener. I'll keep the books for the ranch, deal with registering the rights to the ditch, manage the insurance. I am not a farmer. Despite my resolution, here I am, morning after morning, digging away with my Weasel Weed Popper, trying to stay ahead of the blackberry vines.

FALL

The days grow shorter now, a change accelerated by the end of Daylight Savings. The days of fall seem to shorten faster than the days of spring lengthen. Surely this is an illusion. But the colors of fall make up for any regret. The maple tree in front of Bill W and Lynn's house, the one where Zoe's placenta was planted, blooms scarlet, beyond a simple red. The aspens planted by Fred are golden, as are many of the lower growing understory bushes in the forest.

The gold and red colors make more obvious the number of trees that have grown brown in the drought, in our woods and even more so along the road to town. Despite this damage, one fall pleasure is dealing with the apple harvest. The apples are good this year. Bill C dried many for snacks and we have juiced some. Apple crisps or cobbler are the dessert of choice. But nothing is more satisfying than to line up jars of golden chunky applesauce and ruby apple chutney. Canning is difficult, and it has taken some years to assemble all the equipment that make it feasible. I won't likely make the appeal my grandmother used to, for someone to bring her lugs of apricots and pears, even when she lived with us in the city. We don't put up the quantities of food for the winter that the early ranch families did. But the apples simply arrive on their own schedule and must be dealt with.

There is a great satisfaction in dealing with the harvest in at least a small way. Bill W is up to his belly button in pumpkins again this year, so we have taken locally grown pumpkins down to the grandchildren for carving, and both pumpkin soup and pumpkin pie grace our community dinners. It all tastes like fall as well as looks like fall around here.

Many of the birds in the neighborhood change with the seasons as well, marking the change in the landscape. All spring and summer we were graced with a little troop of Anna's hummingbirds. Their busy feeding and aggressive behavior to fend off other birds as well as people were endlessly fascinating. Unlike last winter, they seem to have left for lower elevations. It is comforting to know that they have moved on for the season, not least since it may mean they believe we will have a more typical winter this year. We had an occasional Calliope hummingbird this summer as well, very small and apparently very irritating to their Anna's cousins. The seed-eating Oregon juncos are back as well, flitting close to the ground and only here for a short time as they move down toward the valley for the winter. We seem to be the middle of their range – they move lower in winter and higher in summer.

Like all the other beasts of the neighborhood, we are beginning to hunker down for the winter: stacking up books to read, lining up jars of applesauce to eat, practicing soup and stew recipes.

Epilogue

As I compiled these stories about a lifetime of challenge and change, our larger neighborhood of Northern California faced unprecedented disasters in the form of fire. Multiple thousands of acres have burned; thousands of houses have been destroyed along with all the possessions of their residents; dozens of people have died. Winter rains are coming and the burned land and tent cities of survivors face a very uncertain future. These enormous problems have been faced by a community newly united and fiercely committed to a future together. Uncommon heroism by first responders has been matched by uncommon gifts of compassion and real assistance. This outpouring of 'Redding Strong', 'Shasta Strong' and now 'Butte Strong' has taken place in the face of a political climate that is nasty and divided. As difficult as the present may be, I remain optimistic that together, we will thrive in this special home place and in the larger community.

I owe a great debt of gratitude to fellow ranch members. Your willingness to let me share my own peculiar take on our shared history is humbling. To all those who have been a part of this ranch community, thank you. To the members of the Carrie Nation Rises, another thank you, for the laughter and the tears, for the learning and growing together. To all the poverty warriors past and present a special respect, along with a belief that we will prevail.

Writing, at least in my case, has required a whole community of encouragement and support. I owe special appreciation to Teresa Jordan along with Bob and the Yearlong Girls, for your care and critical support in our writing together for that wonderful year. It was the start of this work. Sally, your art work and encouragement have made a huge difference to the final product. Thank you to Kathie, for showing the way with your own work and for your unfailing friendship and support. Thank you to Gail for your own brand of love and your editorial eye. Thank you as well to Jaci for your willingness to read and edit draft after draft.

Always, thank you to Bayliss and Andrew and to Ben and Maria, along with that quintet of fabulous grandchildren, for time together at the ranch, for helping me hone these stories, for hikes and swims and opulent meals in the mountains. Most of all, appreciation to Bill for support, encouragement, and ready offers to cook the meal if it kept the writing going. This has always been a family affair.

New Releases from *River Sanctuary Publishing*

House Calls: Guidance on Common Medical Topics by Terry Hollenbeck, MD. 2019. 304 p. full color. $29.95

The Musings of Consciousness, by David Weiss. 2018. $14.95

Parables & Myths, poetry by Climbing Sun, 2018. $12.95

Co-Creating Prayerful Living, by Unity prayer chaplain Bobbie Spivey. 2018. $9.95

Other Memoirs

Hands and Heart: Stories of General Surgery by Michael DeHaan MD. 2013. $14.95

Path to a Wonderful Life by Orma Hammond. 2015. $11.95

Psyche, Eros and Me: A Mythic Memoir by Deanna McKinstry-Edwards, PhD. 2015. $14.95

The Mountain Man and Me: Memories of an Extraordinary Father by Bobbie Hopkins Spivey. 2017. $12.95

The Vallian Trilogy – An Inventive Life part III: The Geometer by Sharon C. Wahl PhD. 2017. $19.95

River Sanctuary Publishing
P.O. Box 1561
Felton, California 95018
www.riversanctuarypublishing.com
(831) 335-7283

We offer custom book design and production with worldwide availability through print-on-demand, with personalized service and the most author-favorable terms in the industry. Specializing in inspirational, spiritual and self-help books, biography, and memoirs.

www.ingramcontent.com/pod-product-compliance
Lightning Source LLC
Chambersburg PA
CBHW060904280326
41934CB00007B/1176